MY HAPPY LIFE FOR SALE

laura taufisiol

To my parents the brightest guiding lights

Copyright © 2017 Laura Paulisich
Photographs copyright © 2017 Laura Paulisich
www.laurapaulisich.com www.myhappylifeforsale.com

All rights reserved.
First Printing, 2017
ISBN 978-0-998-18993-2

Design by Laura Paulisich

Ten years ago I set out on a quest to be the healthiest human I could possibly be.
I had no idea I would become the happiest being I have ever been!

It all started when I became determined to find out what humans need nutritionally. Learning about nutrition led to learning about sleep; learning about sleep led to learning about skin: "It's not only what we eat but also what we touch"(Dr Josh Axe). Life transformed drastically: toxin-free food, clothing, shoes, bedding, towels, mattress, shampoo, cleaners, toothpaste and eventually everything.

Every action I took to become the healthiest human possible produced the happiest feelings I have ever experienced. The transformation from relying on industrialized products to procuring ingredients from nature reignited the health and happiness that are birthrights. Unbuyable, the solutions to survive and thrive reside deep within us all. *My Happy Life for Sale* is a blueprint for cultivating health and happiness by inputting impeccable ingredients to output enlightened enjoyment. H E L L O !   H A P P I N E S S

I used to be "normal:" television watching; yo-yo dieting; stressed about weight, health, and food; unsure how to prepare food and what exactly to eat; always hungry; always thinking about food; always confused about food (what to buy and how to prepare it); shopping; spending; discarding of spoiled food and unworn clothes, unread books, unused belongings; stressing about credit card debts; constantly shopping for food, clothing, belongings, books; rearranging belongings; throwing away excess belongings; collapsing on the couch; zoning out with television; feeling lost, confused, wasteful, wanting, stressed, unsatisfied, and sometimes depressed.

Now that I have discovered a new way of living, I have spent several years without any of those feelings and behaviors! By discovering a purpose for eating, wearing, and living, I gained clarity, equanimity and joy. Today my life is extremely different! I have no tv, no couch, no diets, no yo-yo weight changes, no waste, no unnecessary debt, no stress! Instead I have freedom, fun, happiness and joy. My life is filled with the most nutritious and delicious food, endless energy, the softest and most comfortable clothing and bedding, inspiring surroundings, pure smells, spirit-filled living and enriching activities. H E L L O !   H A P P I N E S S

SLEEP....................15

FOOD....................29

CLOTHING...............83

SHELTER................115

SPIRIT..................147

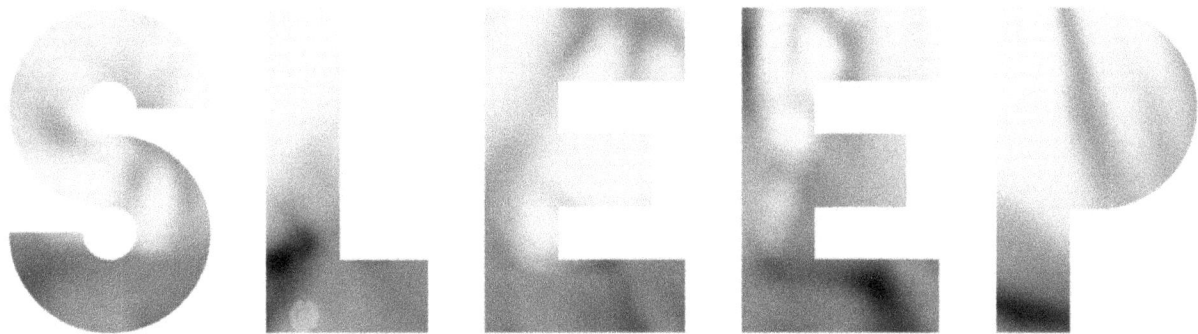

Realizing the impact sleep has on life and well-being has been one of the most significant discoveries! Learning that sleep affects weight, the cells, brain function, spirit, energy, health and happiness, I now consider it the most crucial action of my day and life. I know with certainty the day will end at an established time in order to be able to sleep for 8-10 hours so that I can wake naturally without an alarm. After reading so many sources about the scientific data of sleep affecting health, I became determined to add this to my diet. I vowed to make this commitment uncompromising. I have been honoring that vow ever since and my happiness has soared! First came creating total darkness: removing all electronics; blocking streetlights (and sometimes sunlight!); blocking lights from appliances; unplugging Wi-Fi. I also started becoming aware of artificial lights and other obstacles for nurturing restorative sleep: I changed home light bulbs to yellow bug lights; installed "f.lux" to my computer for less-harsh monitor light; stopped looking at screens and monitors as sleep time approached. Since making these changes, I have experienced repeated nights of restful and restorative sleep, repeated feelings of extreme comfort and relaxation, repeated feelings of balanced and relaxed appetite, repeated feelings of gratitude and well-being, and repeated feelings of H E L L O !   H A P P I N E S S .

DIY Natural Bedding

From Farm to Bed
local. sustainable. breathable.
clean. chemical free. comfortable.
warm. cool. long lasting. natural.

"The primary filling material used in most conventional mattresses is polyurethane foam — a highly flammable petroleum-based material. Because of its high flammability, polyurethane foam must be treated or wrapped with fire retardant chemicals. Flame-retardant chemicals have been linked to serious health risks, including infertility, birth defects, neurodevelopmental delays, reduced IQ scores and behavioral problems in children, hormone disruptions, and various forms of cancer. The risks may be especially dangerous to children, as research revealed that children born to women who were exposed to high levels of PBDEs during pregnancy had, on average, a 4.5 point decrease in IQ. Such children are also more prone to hyperactivity disorders. Remember, these chemicals don't 'stay put' in the mattress. They migrate out and collect in house dust. As a result, an estimated 90 percent of Americans have some level of flame-retardant chemicals in their bodies." - Dr Mercola

"Artificial light disrupts the body's circadian rhythm—the body's 24-hour sleep/wake cycle—and has been shown to affect things like brain wave patterns, hormone production, and cell regulation. Disrupting this circadian rhythm has also been linked to medical issues like depression, obesity, breast and prostate cancer, and cardiovascular disease. It's even associated with sleep disorders like insomnia and delayed phase sleep disorder...A few small changes can help minimize the problems associated with sleep and artificial light. For starters, don't keep your phone near you when you sleep, and avoid all artificially lit screens (like televisions, iPads, and iPhones) right before bedtime. Shield artificial light properly in the bedroom (by turning your alarm so that the light faces away from you, for example), and use light at night only when it's absolutely needed." - sleep.org

"Your hormone balance, which controls proper cellular function and repair at night, is driven by melatonin. Melatonin is produced when it gets dark, and its production can shut off with just a flash of light."
- Dr Myron Wentz & Dave Wentz

REASONS

"One of the best-kept secrets for restful, rejuvenating sleep is the quality of your experiences during the day. When you live each moment completely and fully appreciate the world around you, you do not accumulate stress; therefore, dynamic daily activity directly benefits the quality of your sleep." - chopra.com

"As a nation, we are sick because we don't sleep. We are fat and diabetic because we don't sleep. We are dying from cancer and heart disease because we don't sleep. An avalanche of peer-reviewed scientific papers supports our conclusion that when we don't sleep in sync with the seasonal variation in light exposure, we fundamentally alter a balance of nature that has been programmed into our physiology since Day One. This cosmic clock is embedded in the physiology of every living thing that exists." - TS Wiley

"...sleep helps enhance your learning and problem-solving skills. Sleep also helps you pay attention, make decisions, and be creative...If you're sleep deficient, you may have trouble making decisions, solving problems, controlling your emotions and behavior, and coping with change. Sleep deficiency also has been linked to depression, suicide, and risk-taking behavior...Sleep helps maintain a healthy balance of the hormones that make you feel hungry (ghrelin) or full (leptin). When you don't get enough sleep, your level of ghrelin goes up and your level of leptin goes down. This makes you feel hungrier than when you're well-rested. Sleep also affects how your body reacts to insulin, the hormone that controls your blood glucose (sugar) level. Sleep deficiency results in a higher than normal blood sugar level, which may increase your risk for diabetes. Sleep also plays a role in puberty and fertility. Your immune system relies on sleep to stay healthy...if you're sleep deficient, you may have trouble fighting common infections" - nhlbi.nih.gov

"If you want to lose weight, get more sleep." - Maria Emmerich

what i do...

1. invest in pure, natural, organic bedding and mattress

2. create total darkness (also avoid artificial light and use yellow light bulbs)

3. cultivate happy sleep through a happy spirit (monitor what I input into my brain during the day)

4. sleep almost always 8-10 hours

5. nightly ritual: homemade organic magnesium spray on my feet and gums

6. monitor the monitor (especially hours before sleep) (install "f.lux" for less harsh screen light)

7. wake naturally without an alarm clock

8. electronics-free bedroom (also unplug Wi-Fi connection before sleeping)

9. consistent routine (repeat, repeat, repeat)

10. COMMITMENT (it takes total discipline and commitment to turn off monitors and to stay true to values with all of the available distractions)

troubleshooting when unable to sleep: keeping eyes closed, staying in bed and continuing total darkness; syncing my breathing with noises or other breathing/snoring; thinking about where outbreath meets inbreath

What I did: bought many, many different kinds of toxin-filled sheets and blankets based on "cuteness" but rarely felt satisfied with any of them; mindlessly watched tv or surfed the Internet too tired to get into bed then set an alarm to force myself awake in time for work; always felt tired; always hit snooze on the alarm; always felt hungry and rarely felt full or satiated; had stressful dreams

REJUVENATING SLEEP RESOURCES

DIY bed and pillows from WWW.DIYNATURALBEDDING.COM (natural rubber slabs to build mattress, organic cotton mattress covers to hold the slabs, organic cotton and wool mattress toppers, organic cotton and wool comforters, organic cotton pillow covers to hold natural-material pillow fillings). I used all of these materials to make a queen-sized bed, a single bed that is also a couch, a dog bed, and a decorative pillow.

Many bedding supplies from WWW.RAWGANIQUE.COM (heirloom colorgrown linen sheets, colorgrown organic cotton flannel sheets, colorgrown organic cotton chenille blankets, colorgrown organic Irish-linen terry blanket, organic wool blankets, made-to-order organic wool and cotton comforter and mattress topper)

Some supplies from WWW.SLEEPNBEAUTY.COM (Mulberry organic silk pillowcases and sheets). I also made a silk sleeping liner for travel (*Buen Camino* book).

Some supplies from WWW.VASTRA.US (Ayurveda colorgrown organic sheets, pillow cases, duvet cover)

Most beloved toxin-free animal skins WWW.ORGANICSHEEPSKINS.COM (small baby-sized rugs/blankets)
WWW.BRAINTAN.COM (Traditional Tanners brain-tanned buffalo robe)

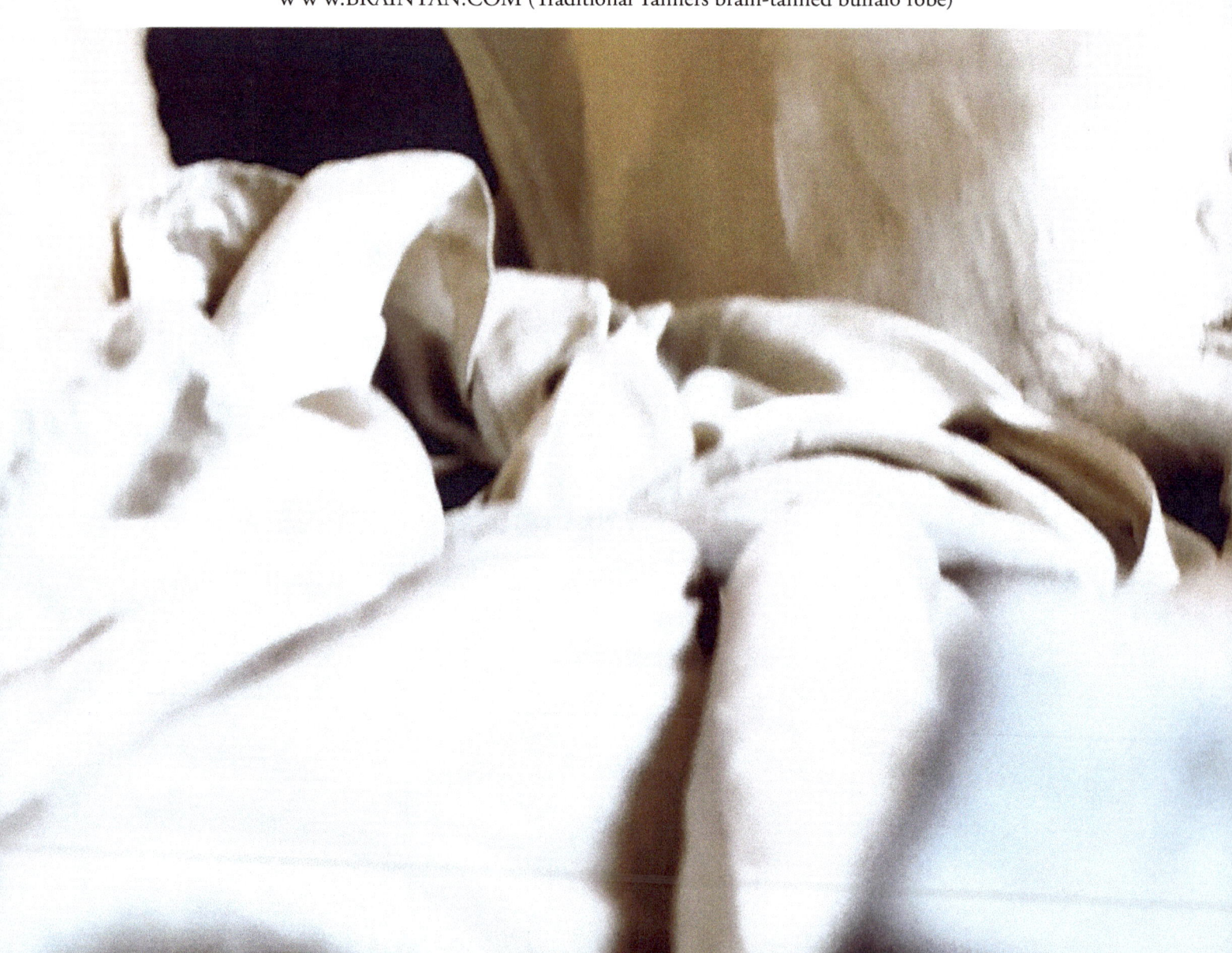

WILDCRAFTED SHEETS

"Our Tulsi bedsheet set is dyed primarily with Holy Basil (Tulsi) which is one of the most powerful known adaptogens helping the body adapt to stress.

100 % Certified Organic Cotton(GOTS certified) 250 thread count Sateen Weave
100% Organically Grown or Wild-Crafted, Sustainably harvested plants and herbs
Main Ingredients in the dyeing concoction: Holy Basilica (Tulsi) 3 types- Krishna, Rama and Vana (truly wild) & Cassiatora linn. Balancing across all Doshas (Ayurvedic Body Types). Other key herbs/plants used: Wild-Crafted Cinnamon (Cinnamomum Zeylanicum), White Turmeric (Curcuma Zedoaria), Diospyros, Eugenia Jombolana, Wild-Crafted Adhatoda Vasica

The use of the Tulsi plant goes back 5000 years in India and it also finds extensive mention in Indian mythology. Known as Holy or Sacred Basil, it is one of the most powerful adaptogens, balancing different processes in the body, and greatly helping one adapt to stress. The Tulsi plant itself is worshiped traditionally in households for protection from illnesses and misery. The leaves of the Tulsi plant are used for treating cough, cold, headaches, stomach disorders, inflammation and many other illnesses." - Vastra

FOOD

The smallest shift in thinking transformed life forever: food is only natural food. By removing processed food as an edible option, I removed all the accompanying fear, confusion, guilt, shame, obsession and stress. After this metamorphosis, I discovered the bliss of providing my body with what it craves: impeccable ingredients from impeccably healthy plants and animals from impeccably healthy soil. It is so easy it is difficult! I lived overwhelmed with all of the "choices" visually permeating the United States. I struggled endlessly every day with trying to "make the right choices." What I didn't realize was by including all of the "food" offered in the United States, I was damaging my physical senses and my emotional psyche with addictive chemicals. I lived in constant confusion and obsession about what to eat. I lived in constant shame and guilt if I indulged in something I knew was "bad." I lived in constant emotional madness of "abstaining" then "giving in" then "remorse." I knew on a deep level that it had to be simple. I longed for peace, equanimity and satiation. By realizing that the purpose of food is to feed our body the nutrients it requires and without those nutrients it will continue to crave and be hungry, I empowered myself with and reignited the health and happiness that are birthrights. Now I live knowing I do my absolute best to provide my body with the most impeccable ingredients possible, and that effort has proven to provide ultimate freedom from any and all outcomes! I have incredible equanimity knowing if anything happens to me, I did everything possible to provide myself with the nutrition humans require. Every day I look back and think "I ate my best," and it creates ultimate equanimity, harmony, and joy. H E L L O !   H A P P I N E S S

"If food were just calories, it wouldn't matter where it came from; as long as it had enough energy to sustain us and tasted good, it would be fine. But the science of nutrition has uncovered a radical new way of looking at food. Food is not just energy. *Food is information.* It contains instructions that communicate messages to your genes, hormones, immune system, gut flora - in fact, to every system of your body. This changes everything we know about food. Health results from the quality of information we put in our bodies."

- Mark Hyman, MD Foreword *The Food Babe*

MEAT *(antelope, beef, bison/buffalo, caribou, deer, elk, goat, lamb, mutton, rabbit)*

FISH AND SHELLFISH *(abalone, anchovy, caviar, clam, crab, crawfish, eel, herring, lobster, mackerel, mussel, octopus, oyster, prawn, perch, salmon, sardine, scallop, shrimp, snail, squid, tuna, walleye)*

HERBS AND SPICES *(balm, basil, bay leaf, chamomile, chervil, chives, cilantro, cinnamon, cloves, curry leaves, dill weed, fennel leaf, fenugreek leaves, galangal, garlic, ginger, horseradish, kaffir lime leaves, lavender, lemon balm, lemongrass, mace, marjoram leaf, mint, oregano leaf, parsley, rosemary, saffron, sage, salt, savory leaf, sea vegetables, tarragon, thyme, turmeric, truffle, vanilla extract)*

LEAFY GREENS *(amaranth greens, arugula, beet greens, bok choy, borage greens, carrot greens, chickweed, chicory, chrysanthemum leaves, collard greens, cress, dandelion, fiddlehead, fluted pumpkin leaves, kale, kohlrabi greens, mizuna, mustard greens, pea leaves, poke, pumpkin sprouts, radicchio, radish sprouts, sea kale, sorrel, spinach, squash blossom, summer purslane, sunflower sprouts, sweet potato greens, Swiss chard, turnip greens, water spinach, watercress, winter purslane)*

EDIBLE INSECTS *(cricket, dragonfly, grasshopper)*

EDIBLE FLOWERS *(calendula, carnation, clover, dandelion, gladiolas, hibiscus, honeysuckle, lavender, marigold, nasturtium, pansy, primrose, scented geranium)*

ROOTS AND TUBERS *(arrowroot, bamboo shoot, ginger, horseradish, wasabi, water chesnut, yacón)*

PROBIOTIC FOODS *(coconut milk kefir yogurt, raw unpasteurized lacto-or wild-fermented vegetables, sauerkraut, and condiments, water kefir, raw cheese, yogurt, kombucha, vegetable kvasses, natto, apple cider vinegar, miso, brine-cured olives)*

BEVERAGES *(bone broth, carbonated water, coconut milk, coconut milk kefir, coconut water, herbal tea: chamomile, chicory, cinnamon, clove, dandelion root, dried fruit, ginger, hibiscus, lavender, lemon balm, marshmallow root, milk thistle, mint, rose hip, rooibos, and turmeric, homemade spa water, lemon or lime juice, mineral water, pickle juice, sauerkraut juice, water/water kefir)*

VITAMINS

Vitamin A *(Retinoids: beef liver, organ meats, goose liver, egg yolks, yellow butter, shellfish, shrimp, fish   Beta Carotene: sweet potatoe, pumpkin, spinach, turnip greens, colored vegetables, green vegetables, cod liver oil & skate oil supplements)*

Thiamin *(pork chops, brown rice, ham, acorn squash, beef steak, liver, heart, kidney, spirulina, asparagus)*

Riboflavin *(meats, green leafy vegetables)*

Niacin *(meat, poultry, fish, mushrooms)*

Pantothenic Acid *(animal organs, chicken, egg yolk, broccoli, mushrooms, avocado)*

Pyridoxine *(meat, fish, poultry)*

Cobalamin *(meat, poultry, fish)*

Biotin *(organ meats, fish)*

Ascorbic Acid/Vitamin C *(lemon & orange, citrus fruits, sweet peppers, broccoli florets, spinach, Brussels sprouts, tomatoes, strawberries, acerola tablets)*

Choline *(liver once/week, salmon, 3 egg yolks/day)*

Calciferol/Vitamin D *(fatty fish, daily sunlight, eggs, dairy products, butterfat, liver/organ meats, marine oils, shrimp, crab)*

Alpha-Tocopherol/Vitamin E *(leafy green vegetables)*

Folic Acid *(liver, giblets, egg yolks, seaweed, green leafy vegetables, mushrooms, beets, nuts, asparagus, spinach, turnip greens, broccoli)*

Vitamin K *(cabbage, liver, goose liver, egg yolks, butter, fermented foods/miso, aged cheese, bone marrow, grains, spinach, broccoli, sprouts, kale, collards, green vegetables)*

MINERALS

Calcium *(sardines, salmon, leafy greens such as broccoli and kale but not Swiss chard or spinach which lessen calcium, dairy products, bone broth with added collagen-rich ox hooves, oxtails, and chicken feet)*

Chloride *(salt/sodium chloride, celery, coconut)*

Chromium *(meat, poultry, fish)*

Copper *(liver, 1/4 pound beef or lamb liver/week, shellfish, nuts, seeds, whole-grain products, beans, prunes, cocoa, black pepper)*

Flouride *(marine fish, teas)*

Iodine *(seafood)*

Iron *(red meat, poultry, green vegetables)*

Magnesium *(beef, chicken, salmon, fish, fish broth, green leafy vegetables, coriander, spinach, chard, broccoli, halibut, pumpkin seeds, whole grains, nuts and seeds, legumes, avocados)*

Manganese *(fish, tea)*

Molybdenum *(deficiencies are rare)*

Phosphorus *(meat, fish, poultry, liver, broccoli)*

Potassium *(meat, vegetables, green leafy vegetables, avocado, beets, sun-dried tomatoes, tubers, meat, milk, many fruits, nuts, grains)*

Selenium *(organ meats, kidneys, goose liver, eggs, fish, seafood, butter, sometimes plants depending on soil quality, beef depending on soil quality, Brazil nuts from selenium-rich Brazilian soils, grains grown in selenium-rich soil)*

Sodium *(salt, vegetables, meat, broth, zucchini)*

Sulfur *(meat, fish, poultry, eggs, milk, cruciferous vegetables)*

Zinc *(7 oysters each week, red meat, fish, poultry, some seafood, ginger, nuts, seeds)*

"Crops (and livestock) are products of their environment, and how they are raised determines what nutrition they ultimately provide. It is well known that there can be considerable variation in protein content, vitamins, and minerals, for example, depending on the soil, the amount of irrigation, the time of harvesting, and the storage period." - Dr Pitcairn

"High levels of heart disease are associated with **selenium**-deficient soil in Finland and a tendency to fibrotic heart lesions is associated with selenium deficiency in parts of China." - Weston Price Foundation

"**Selenium** content of foods can vary dramatically depending on the Selenium content of local soils. Livestock raised in western Canada have four times more selenium than livestock raised in eastern Canada...One pound of beef might provide anywhere from 86 to 985 micrograms of selenium!...Brazil nuts from other locations [places other than high-selenium Brazilian soils] may have much less selenium." - Paul Jaminet and Shou-Ching Jaminet

"Excessive use of salt along with inadequate intake of fruits and vegetables can result in a **potassium** deficiency." Weston Price Foundation

"Lacto-fermented beverages and bone broths both provide easily assimilated **chloride**. Other sources include celery and coconut." - Weston Price Foundation

"High **magnesium** levels in drinking water have been linked to resistance to heart disease. Although it is found in many foods, including dairy products, nuts, vegetables, fish, meat and seafood, deficiencies are common in America due to soil depletion, poor absorption and lack of minerals in drinking water. A diet high in carbohydrates, oxalic acid in foods like raw spinach and phytic acid found in whole grains can cause deficiencies. High amounts of zinc and vitamin D increase magnesium requirements. Magnesium deficiency can result in coronary heart disease, chronic weight loss, obesity, fatigue, epilepsy and impaired brain function. Chocolate cravings are a sign of magnesium deficiency." - Weston Price Foundation

"More than half of the **copper** in foods is absorbed. Nuts, molasses and oats contain copper but liver is the best and most easily assimilated source. Copper deficiency is widespread in America. Animal experiments indicate that copper deficiency combined with high fructose consumption has particularly deleterious effects on infants and growing children." - Weston Price Foundation

"Eskimo groups - who for thousands of years have eaten virtually no plant foods for most of the year - didn't get scurvy...they got their **vitamin C** from other natural sources - raw fish, seal, and caribou." - Loren Cordain

"We have to eat eight oranges to get the same amount of **vitamin C** as our grandparents got from eating just one. Despite all of our advances in technology and agricultural practices, the health of our soil is only getting worse. Our soil today has 85 percent fewer minerals than it contained 100 years ago...Aggressive agricultural methods have literally stripped the minerals and nutrients out of the soil...the industry has defaulted to fast-growing, pest-resistant production, making every generation of produce less nutritious than the last. All over the world, minerals and nutrients in our soil have been lost because of these farming practices. Some estimate that only forty-eight years of nutrient-rich topsoil remains." - Dr Josh Axe

"In some ways, **minerals** are more essential to our health than vitamins. Our bodies can't manufacture minerals, so we must get them from our diet. The minerals in food are supplied by the soil where the produce was grown. Healthy soil also helps to supply specific vitamins, natural antibiotics, amino acids, and phytochemicals vital to our health. Some of our worst chronic illnesses stem from nutritional deficiencies: heart disease, stroke, diabetes, obesity, bone loss, high blood pressure, dementia, macular degeneration, and leaky gut... Historically, entire civilizations have died off when their topsoil was depleted of nutrients." - Dr Josh Axe

Semi-annual food shopping: drive 30 minutes to butcher shop to pick up Valley Graze or 3D Farm whole beef

ALIMENT

noun | al·i·ment | \ˈa-le-ment \

1 : food; nourishment

verb

1 : provide with nourishment or sustenance

"When you go into a supermarket in the United States, there is hardly any food!...There was not a lot, in most American supermarkets, that most French people would consider (traditionally at least) an *aliment* ('a nourishment')...the processed and prepared foods that filled up the aisles in a North American grocery store weren't real food, because, although they were edible, they weren't nourishing." - Karen Lebillon

No Farms No Food

American Farmland Trust
www.farmland.org

FOOD VS INDUSTRIALIZED FOOD

"Year by year the food we eat is becoming more and more like Doritos...the food companies, whose profit is directly related to the amount of food people eat, have been quietly amping up the amounts of salt, sugar, and fat in our foods, and the results are obvious." - Mark Schatzker

"Amazingly, we've become a culture that considers Twinkies, Cocoa Puffs, and Mountain Dew safe, but raw milk and compost-grown tomatoes unsafe." - Joel Salatin

"I wondered how the approximately one hundred thousand synthetic chemical molecules that have invaded our environment and our dinner plates for a half century are evaluated and regulated...is there a link between exposure to these chemical substances and the spectacular increase in cancers, neurodegenerative diseases, reproductive disorders, diabetes, and obesity that have been recorded in developed countries, to such a degree that the World Health Organization speaks of an 'epidemic'?" - Marie-Monique Robin

"Dr Amy Reichenbach: new scientific research shows that our brains and bodies often become physically addicted to factory foods. In fact, sugar seems to stimulate the brain's reward centers with the neurotransmitter dopamine exactly like other addictive drugs do. In short, research is showing that we may need to literally 'detox' off factory foods the same way we would addictive drugs." - Christine Avanti

"Dr Leila Denmark was the world's oldest active pediatrician when she retired at the age of 103; she recently died at age 114...At her 100th birthday she refused cake because it had sugar in it, and at her 103rd birthday party, when she again refused cake, she explained that she hadn't eaten any food made with sugar for seventy years."
- Paul Jaminet PhD & Shou-Ching Jaminet PhD

"Food is like a language, an unbroken information stream that connects every cell in your body to an aspect of the natural world...If you eat a properly cooked steak from an open-range, grass-fed cow, then you are receiving information not only about the health of that cow's body, but about the health of the grasses from which it ate, and the soil from which those grasses grew. If you want to know whether or not a steak, or a fish, or a carrot is good for you, ask yourself what portions of the natural world it represents, and whether or not the bulk of that information remains intact. This requires traveling backwards down the food chain, step by step, until you reach the ground or the sea." - Catherine Shanahan MD & Luke Shanahan

"The food you eat is making you sick and the agencies that are providing you with guidelines on what to eat are giving dangerous advice with devastating health consequences. You can change that today." - Dr William Davis cardiologist

"Minerals are lost in the treatment of drinking water. Water was the largest source of calcium and magnesium in Paleolithic diets, but modern water treatment removes most dissolved minerals." - Paul Jaminet PhD & Shou-Ching Jaminet PhD

"*Chemical contamination* of the food chain is an increasing problem that is becoming a major factor in chronic disease, particularly for animals. It is difficult for us to comprehend just how frequently these chemicals appear in food. The process starts with the herbicides, insecticides, and fungicides used to grow crops. Despite Rachel Carson's landmark warning about the dangers of pesticides, today we use produce pesticides at a rate 13,000 times greater than we did in 1962, the year that her book *Silent Spring* first appeared. The process continues with antibiotics, growth stimulants, hormones, tranquilizers, and other drugs fed to livestock consuming grains." - Dr Pitcairn

"No diet that we can formulate from least-cost products and process for convenience and long storage can ever rival those mysteriously complex fresh-food diets offered for eons by Nature herself." - Dr Pitcairn

what i do...

1. Food = plants and animals made by the healthiest nature I can find. That's it! Once I removed industrialized foods from the food category my life changed forever! Hello! Happiness. I didn't realize how much stress and anxiety I had around food until I retrained my brain to its birthright of eating natural food.

2. Finding natural food can be challenging! I get all my food from WWW.EATWILD.COM or The Weston Price Foundation Shopping Guide. Even then I speak directly to the farmers and ask many, many questions.

3. Always eat and cook plants and animals with a generous amount of the healthiest, natural fat I can find.

4. Consider the diets of the animals; consider the soil of the plants; consider the soil of the plants for the diets of the animals.

5. Came to believe and know: I-will-always-be-hungry-if-I-don't-eat-the-necessary-nutrients.

6. Intermittent Fasting (IM): the natural fats keep me full, satiated, and nourished for many, many hours (I frequently eat one meal a day).

7. Transdermal consideration (I consider the "nutrition" of everything I put on my skin).

8. Chew until food is liquid for the absorption of nutrients.

9. Low-temperature cooking in natural, unglazed cookware to retain nutrients.

10. Whole-food supplements (cod liver oil, skate liver oil, alma tablets, turmeric, emu oil, Azomite powder).

"The proper way to take in minerals is through mineral-rich water; through nutrient-dense foods and beverages; through mineral-rich bone broths in which all of the macrominerals—sodium, chloride, calcium, magnesium, phosphorus, potassium and sulphur—are available in ready-to-use ionized form as a true electrolyte solution; through the use of unrefined sea salt; and by adding small amounts of fine clay or mud as a supplement to water or food, a practice found in many traditional societies throughout the world. Analysis of clays from Africa, Sardinia and California reveals that clay can provide a variety of macro- and trace minerals including calcium, phosphorus, magnesium, iron and zinc. Clay also contains aluminum, but silicon, present in large amounts in all clays, prevents absorption of this toxic metal and actually helps the body eliminate aluminum that is bound in the tissues." - Weston Price Foundation

"A study of high school kids in Massachusetts found that ninth- and tenth-grade girls who drank soda were far more likely to suffer broken bones than girls who didn't drink any." - Eric Schlosser & Charles Wilson

"The essential causes of tooth decay have been known to the modern world for approximately eight years. Harvard Professor Earnest Hooton clearly and succinctly summarized the problem: 'It is store food that has given us store teeth.' Timothy Gallagher DDS says, 'If you are susceptible to tooth decay, stay away from all sweet fruits; many of them have all been hybridized to make them as sweet as possible.' Homemade broths are one of the most potent medicines for tooth decay (1-2 cups/day as tea, soups, stews or gravy)." - Ramiel Nagel

"Sally Fallon: when broth is cooled, it congeals due to the presence of gelatin. The use of gelatin as a therapeutic agent goes back to the ancient Chinese...although gelatin is not a complete protein, containing only the amino acids agrinine and glycine in large amounts, it acts as a protein sparer, helping the poor stretch a few morsels of meat into a complete meal. During the siege of Paris, when vegetables and meat were scarce, a doctor named Guerard put his patients on gelatin bouillon with some added fat and they survived in good health." - Kristen Michaelis

Turmeric: "My mother used daily in virtually every meal. She'd also sprinkle it on a cut when I fell and hurt myself. Or put it on my forehead when I had a fever. If I was nauseaous, she gave me ginger to make me feel better." Ayurveda: "India's system of natural healing, which employs spices, herbs, and healthful lifestyle to prevent and treat disease." - *Healing Spices* by Bharat B. Aggarwal, PhD

"Only the finest Organic, Grade 10 quality Indian turmeric is ground in Premier Research Lab's non-toxic grinder and then immediately encapsulated in 100% vegetable capsules without any toxic excipients whatsoever. No magnesium stearate (a hydrogenated oil), talcum or silicon dioxide (ground sand) are used. Immediate encapsulation helps trap and preserve the complete spectrum of phytochemicals indigenous to well-grown nutraceuticals. Quantum Turmeric and all raw materials used by PRL, must pass photoluminescent near-infrared spectrum analysis to ensure that all raw materials are non-irradiated and not contaminated with pesticide/insecticide residues. Premier Turmeric can be taken daily in capsule form or can be enjoyed as an everyday spice you add to your food. Whichever way turmeric is consumed, it will provide many wonderful benefits, especially for those with health issues related to inflammation, digestive issues, and skin issues. Also, it should be noted that turmeric's magical properties are further liberated in a matrix of oil, so it is recommended that it first be mixed with olive, sesame – or our favorite – organic coconut – oil before being taken. It does not have to be sautéed or cooked, but merely blended."
- Radiant Life Catalog

"Found in turmeric, curcumin has previously been shown to have anti-inflammatory and antioxidant properties in lab studies. It also has been suggested as a possible reason that senior citizens in India, where curcumin is a dietary staple, have a lower prevalence of Alzheimer's disease and better cognitive performance." - newsroom.ucla.edu

THE SKINNY ON FAT

1. Eating healthy fat creates happiness! The satiation, increased energy, brain care and resolution of health problems create better mental health including a positive and optimistic view of life.

2. By feeding my body what it needs (nutrients and fat), hunger and cravings are eliminated. If I ever find myself hungry I always investigate my diet to ensure proper nutrients and fat consumption.

3. Healthy, traditional fats include pork lard, beef/lamb/bison fat, butter, ghee, meat fats, egg yolks, traditionally-made olive oil, coconut oil and cod-liver oil.

4. Costa Rica, famous for many centenarians, reports families of 7-8 people butchering one pig a month and rendering 5 gallons of fat (that is almost 1 gallon of fat per person per month).

5. Masai tribes drink at least a gallon of milk per day (3/4 of a pound of butterfat a day) and consume 4-10 pounds of meat at a festival.

6. 60% of the brain is fat. Eating healthy fat feeds the brain.

7. Eating healthy fat feeds our cells for proper cell functioning.

8. Coconut oil increases metabolism!

9. Obesity is a sign that that person's cells are more sensitive to insulin (carbohydrates) than other people's cells.

10. "If you have a weight problem it is not your fault!" - Gary Taubes (Get rid of the carbs! Don't eat the foods that make you fat! The leanest you can be is on the diet with the fewest carbohydrates.)

HOW I USE FAT

coconut oil - liver snaps, pan frying, sauces, melt like butter, dog food topping, dessert, skin care

olive oil - salad dressing, cold sauces, like melted butter, skin care

palm oil - pan frying special recipes

almond oil - massage oil, skin care

avocado oil - salad dressing, cold sauces, skin care

walnut oil - wood sealer

beef/bison/lamb fat - deep frying, pan frying, leg-of-lamb (pour melted fat over marinating and roasting meat)

IF I COULD FIND (naturally-fed) PORK, CHICKEN AND DUCK

pork fat - pan frying, liver snaps, mayonnaise, pâté

bacon fat - mayonnaise, pâté

duck fat - special occasions! roasting whole chicken and/or chicken wings

THE GREASY DIET

"The traditional diet of Okinawa consists of white rice, sweet potatoes, fish, pork, eggs, and vegetables, including seaweed. All parts of pigs were eaten ('tails to nails'), and lard was used for cooking. The gerontologist Kazuhiko Taira described traditional Okinawan food as 'very, very greasy.'

On these foods Okinawans had the longest life expectancy in the world, with numerous centenarians. The age-adjusted death rate from heart disease was 82 percent lower than in the United States, from cancer 27 percent lower, and from all causes 36 percent lower. Hormone-dependent cancers, such as breast, ovarian, and colon cancer, were 50 to 80 percent less frequent in Okinawa than in the United States.

Centenarians had the highest intake of milk, meat, fish, eggs, fat, and oils.

Unfortunately, Okinawans recently began to eat vegetable oils, grains, and industrially prepared foods. Okinawans now have widespread obesity, rising rates of heart disease, cancer, and diabetes, and shortening life span."

- Paul Jaminet and Shou-Ching Jaminet, *Perfect Health Diet*

Butter-colored rendered bison fat! (100% grassfed bison raised on native grasses from pristine soil)

Eating fat does not make me fat! This lesson took me several years to trust. I had to retrain my brain with every tentative bite of fat I allowed myself to eat. Slowly, very s l o w l y, I learned that eating healthy, mindfully-sourced fat does not make me fat. Actually, the complete opposite happens. For the first time in my life, I felt full, satisfied, satiated, H A P P Y after eating rather than hungry and ashamed of looking for more. For the first time in my life, I felt calm, peaceful, and alert after eating and the stress of still being hungry had disappeared. For the first time in my life, I enjoyed eating and became so grateful for every delicious morsel of food I find and prepare.

I remember reading while searching for nutrition answers that when eating nutrient-dense foods it does not take much food to sustain humans. I found this to be true!

I become full and stay full when eating high fat with modest protein and low carbs. In the Spring 2017 issue of *Wise Traditions*, Thomas S. Cowan, MD, writes about there not being an internal mechanism that tells us to stop eating carbs the way that excess fat and protein do. I found this to be true also!

I used to be able to eat almost a whole box of cereal! I would read the box and the serving information while I was eating and wonder, "How can I not be full after eating one serving?!" I felt so ashamed!

The same was true for cake, candy, doughnuts (on and on...). I always felt so stressed that I would eat everything and not be able to stop!

Now life is so much different. Magically and unbelievably, every day during eating high healthy-fat and some protein, I get to a point where I want to stop. I overwhelmingly feel as though I want to stop eating; my hunger just disappears. H E L L O ! H A P P I N E S S

INTERMITTANT FASTING

"Sixteen hours is the optimal length for fasts. This is short enough that it is possible to repeat the fast daily but long enough to induce elevated levels of autophagy. In animals, daily fasting for sixteen hours with an eight-hour feeding window delivers significant health benefits. Populations that fast are noted for their good health and longevity."
Perfect Health Diet Paul Jaminet, PhD & Shou-Ching Jaminet, PhD

WHAT'S IN THE FRIDGE?
23 October 2017 Hudson, Wisconsin USA
Latitude 44.97°N

local horseradish root

local Swiss chard

local spinach

local watercress

backyard parsley

backyard mint

backyard lemon balm

backyard sage

backyard garlic chives

backyard nasturtium

backyard lavender

backyard rue

homemade alcohol-free vanilla extract

homemade bone broth

homemade lacto-fermented pickles

wildcrafted organic witch hazel, honeysuckle hydrosol, pine cone extract (www.organicwitchhazel.com)

organic Moroccan rose water for cooking (www.amazon.com)

homemade skin-nourishing massage oil

homemade grass-fed rendered beef fat

homemade grass-fed rendered bison fat

vanilla-infused coconut oil

traditionally-fermented cod liver oil & skate liver oil (www.radiantlifecatalog.com)

What used to be in the fridge: industrially-produced salad dressing, mustard, skim milk, prepackaged baby carrots, apples, oranges, kiwi, green peppers, cauliflower, broccoli, rotisserie chicken, shredded low-fat cheese, parmesan cheese in a can all purchased at a large, conventional grocery chain. I also had many "food" items in the cupboards: pasta, low-fat chips, low-fat crackers, french bread, whole wheat bread, boxed cereal, "health food" energy bars, low-fat frosting. Now, I don't have cupboards! The only foods I keep on the counter are salt, basil, herb plants, dried anchovies, coconut oil, coconut cream, shredded coconut, jerky, and sometimes rendered fat.

FRESH HERBS

I wonder why these little gems don't get more media attention!

I have been asked on several occasions, in several different markets, in several different locations, and by several different sellers or other customers the same question: "what will you do with all of those herbs?"

From this recurring experience I assume that:

1. most customers are not purchasing solely herbs and leafy greens in their baskets

2. most people don't think of herbs as "legitimate" fruits and vegetables

3. most people are unfamiliar with herbs

For the majority of my life I did not know about fresh herbs! I didn't even know fruits and vegetables were carbohydrates!

Now I eat fresh herbs almost every day and am in love with the bitter and beautiful taste of fresh herbs from the garden grown from heirloom, non-G.M.O., organic seeds! HELLO! HAPPINESS

WHOLE FOOD SUPPLEMENTS

Premier Turmeric (sprinkled into olive oil with sea salt - drink, dip, or dressing)
emu oil (teaspoon)
amla tablets (10 daily)
cod liver oil (tablespoon)
skate oil (teaspoon)
Azomite mineral powder (1-2 teaspoons mixed into bone broth)
probiotic (few times a week)
ox bile and pancreatic enzyme (with meals)

SUPERFOODS

Azomite mineral powder (*an excellent source of silica, calcium, magnesium and the gamut of trace minerals. Clay also has detoxifying effects as the negatively charged clay particles attract positively charged pathogens and take them out of the body...Take a heaping teaspoon mixed with water daily as an insurance of adequate macro- and trace mineral ingestion in these days of soil depletion through intensive farming." - Weston Price Foundation*)
bee pollen
spirulina ("*The Aztecs ate it as a staple food, dried and spread on tortillas. Africans of the Sahara region also use dried spirulina with grains and vegetables. These algae are high in protein, carotenoids and minerals." - Weston Price Foundation*)
bitters ("*Herbal extracts of bitter, mineral-rich herbs are a traditional tonic for stimulating the bile and increasing digestion and assimilation of fats. They often are the best remedy for calming a queasy stomach. One such product is made by Floradix. Another is Swedish Bitters originally formulated by Paracelsus and later 'rediscovered' by a Swedish scientist. Bitters supply nutrients from bitter leaves that are often lacking in the Western diet. Many cultures, including the Chinese and Hindu, value bitter herbs for their cleansing, strengthening and healing properties." - Weston Price Foundation*)
cod liver oil
evening primrose oil, borage oil and black current oil
small daily supplement of kelp tablet or powder
noni juice on an empty stomach

"Even those who live in isolated primitive societies seek out special foods for optimum health—foods high in fat-soluble vitamins, such as fish eggs and organ meats, to ensure reproduction and strong healthy children; soaked grains for strength and stamina; and herbs to prevent certain diseases." - Weston Price Foundation

I grew up in the U.S. learning about food and "cooking" from the television. This is what I ate and prepared:

-a lot of boxed cereal with skim milk

-a lot of raw fruit and vegetables dipped in low-fat salad dressing purchased from the store

-some yogurt, french bread, nuts, raisins, dried fruit, bites of cheese, little bites of peanut butter (store-bought)

-sometimes store-bought rotisserie chicken still hot, "homemade" soup from the co-op (heat in the microwave)

-sometimes pasta with lean ground beef mixed with cheese

-sometimes brown rice with microwave-steamed frozen vegetables sprinkled with canned parmesan cheese

-phases of low-fat tortilla chips topped with low-fat/fat-free cheese (microwave-melted) and low-fat salsa from a jar

-phases of energy bars with "healthy" ingredients (peanuts, peanut butter, cereal, raisins, honey, pumpkin seeds)

-phases of low-fat "healthy" crackers

cheating: cake, chips, soda, fat-free candy, low-fat candy, candy, restaurant appetizers, movie theater popcorn with movie theater butter-flavored topping

This was the majority of my life. The whole time I was eating like this and having no idea how to cook, I was always wondering about, thinking about, pretty much obsessed about food and cooking. I even purchased (but didn't ever use) many expensive stand mixers, blenders, pans, tools and even watched cooking shows!

I felt lost and confused.

Now, the more I do to stay alive (eat only real food, wear only toxin-free clothes and shoes, sleep 8-10 hours in a completely dark and electronics-free bedroom and toxin-free bed) the more joy I feel.

It is also true for me that in all my studying and searching, something just clicked for me. Food products being sold, marketed, and displayed in grocery stores do not meet my qualifications for being considered food.

People from other countries can easily recognize this: "US grocery stores have no food!" But for me who learned from television that breakfast is boxed cereal with skim milk and that food is sold in grocery stores, it took a MIRACLE to realize it!

"Eat real food whose flavor tells the gripping story of its nutrition...In nature, flavor never appears without nutrition. No morsel of food should pass your lips before you have asked the following question: where did the flavor come from? If it came from the plant or animal you're eating, keep eating. If it was applied by a human with a PhD in chemistry, put it down." - Mark Schatzker

WHY I DON'T EAT IN RESTAURANTS

How would I know what I'm eating?! Unless it is a very special restaurant, how will I know:

the breed of the animal?

if the animal was born on the farm?

the daily life and health of the animal?

EVERYTHING the animal ate during its life?

the history of the animal's parents?

what the soil is like?

what kind of vegetation is on the farm?

the health of the vegetation?

what are the farming practices of the neighboring farm?

the methods for processing the animal?

the age of the animal?

the age of the meat?

the fats used to cook?

the salt used to cook?

the cookware surfaces used to cook?

the temperature and time used to cook?

REASONS

"Your body manufactures 2,000,000 red blood cells every second; just look at what you ate and drank in the past 24 hours to see what your new red blood cells are made of!" - Paul Chek

"By cutting down on the toxins entering your body from poor food and drink choices and by reducing the amount of sugar in your diet, you'll see a dramatic difference. If you eat organic, free range [grass-fed] meats, you don't have to worry about cutting the fat away and you can eat red meats. In no time, you'll have more energy, your cholesterol levels are likely to normalize, and you'll be far more interested in getting the exercise you need…you'll look and feel at least ten years younger!" - Paul Chek

"[As found in Ancel Keys' 1950s study of seven countries] the least amount of heart disease was on the island of Crete, where the predominently rural population ate a huge amount of meat. The balance of their caloric intake consisted of grain, fruit, and vegetables, along with a staggering amount of olive oil - it accounted for forty percent of their diets. For the farmers there, it was literally a beverage. They actually drank it for breakfast…[they] had no processed or packaged foods, no electricity, and no stress…they ate real food, walked a lot, went to bed when it got dark, got up when it was light, took care of their own children, and didn't worry about 'keeping up with the Strovropopouloses.'" - TS Wiley with Bent Formby PhD

"Many of our grandparents and great-grandparents also recognized the power of food, feeding their families organ meats and spooning out cod liver oil. Somehow this knowledge has slowly faded away, while processed foods have taken center stage." - Katherine Erlich MD & Kelly Genzlinger CNC CMTA

"[Weston Price] concluded: the common denominator of good health was to eat a traditional diet consisting of fresh foods from animals and plants grown on soils that were themselves rich in nutrients." - Michael Pollan

"All of us - humans and animals - should have a variety of fresh, wholesome, unprocessed food…Europeans feed their dogs much more naturally…Many breeders have commented…that such European dogs are far healthier than American dogs. No diet that we can formulate from least-cost products and process for convenience and long storage can ever rival those mysteriously complex fresh-food diets offered for eons by Nature herself." - Dr Pitcairn

"Plants (vegetables, fruits, nuts, seeds, and herbs/spices) and animals (meat, fish, fowl and eggs) should represent the entire composition of your diet." - Mark Sisson

"Eat the right foods: meat, seafood, roots and tubers, leafy vegetables, eggs, fruit and nuts. Experiment with full-fat fermented dairy. Aim for a diet where the bulk of calories comes from seafood and animals, but the physical bulk comes from plants. Don't be afraid of fat, eat nose to tail, and eat a variety of plants. Respect ancient culinary wisdom. Follow traditional recipes. Eat fermented foods. Eat raw foods. Make broths and stocks. Cook at low heat, using traditional fats and oils (coconut, beef, butter, ghee, olive). Lead a healthy lifestyle. Sleep as much as possible. Move and exercise regularly. Stay on your feet (stand, walk, run). Get regular, moderate sun. Try some intermittent fasting. Try some hot and cold exposure. Make it meaningful in order to make it an ongoing lifestyle." - John Durant

"Many people believe that diet has little to do with mental or emotional health. Yet hundreds of research studies prove that nutrient deficiencies and imbalances adversely affect the way we think and feel. After all, the brain and the nervous system are integral parts of our physical bodies and need to be nourished, just like the other organs. With a healthy body and brain, we can produce the endorphins and other biochemical compounds needed to feel optimistic, happy, balanced and focused. These 'feel-good' chemicals not only equip us to become high functioning individuals able to cope with the stresses of daily life, but also help those who've suffered psychological wounds and traumas." - www.westonprice.org/health-topics/mental-health-flyer-references/

"Ounce for ounce, liver may contain more nutrients than any other food."

MIRACULOUS MICROGREENS

"mineral malnutrition is considered to be one of the most important global challenges to mankind that can be prevented and is one of the Millennium Development Goals...With respect to nutrition, the flaws in food systems create a dichotomous problem of excess and insufficiency. This is exemplified by one-third of the world's people being overweight and/or undernourished...This problem impacts countries of every economic status...The reliance of urban populations on long food chains limits accessibility to produce that has short shelf lives and, therefore, poor transportability, and increases dependence on heavily processed and packaged foods; this creates 'food deserts' in urban areas in which people do not have ready access to a complete compliment of required nutrients...However, even the fresh produce that does reach its destination has likely lost substantial nutritional value during transport...a newly emerging crop that may be a dense source of nutrition in the absence of biofortification and genetic engineering and has the potential to be produced in just about any locale is microgreens. Microgreens are edible seedlings that are usually harvested 7–14 days after germination when they have two fully developed cotyledon leaves...A wide variety of herbs (e.g., basil, cilantro), vegetables (e.g., radish, broccoli, and mesclun) and even flowers (e.g., sunflowers) are grown as microgreens. Microgreens are generally more flavorful, some of them quite spicy, than their mature counterparts and have grown in popularity among culinary artists for adding texture and flavor accents to salads, sandwiches, and other dishes...The increasing culinary demand as well as the ease with which microgreens can be grown, even by inexperienced gardeners in urban settings, has piqued interests in growing and eating them...**microgreens may have 4–40 times the amount of some nutrients and vitamins as the vegetables a mature plant would produce...**the nutritional aspects they measured varied widely among microgreen types...Additionally...the methods used to grow microgreens (i.e., soil, compost, hydroponic) can significantly impact their nutritional value...The relatively high nutritional value of broccoli microgreens compared to the vegetable is consistent with previous studies reporting that produce at early growth stages (i.e., sprouts, microgreens, 'baby' vegetables) are denser sources of nutrition than their mature counterparts. It has been noted that vegetables, especially when grown on nutrient poor soils, have low mineral concentrations. Fertilization of nutrient poor soils can increase mineral concentration in plant leaves, but not always in the produce that is consumed because minerals are not distributed evenly in all plant parts...simply increasing fertilizer application does not represent a viable solution for improving the nutritional value of crops and simultaneously has negative consequences on the environment. Additionally, fertilizer manufacturing is no longer sustainable at current rates. In this context, the potential to grow microgreens themselves without the use of fertilizer application is intriguing." - https://www.ncbi.nlm.nih.gov/pmc/articles/PMC5362588/

Broccoli - Purple Sprouting Microgreens: antioxidants, fiber, Vitamins A, C, and B-complex, calcium, potassium and copper

Radish - Hong Vit Microgreens: Vitamins A, B, C, E, & K, folic acid, niacin, potassium, iron, phosphorus, pantothenic acid, calcium, magnesium, zinc, carotenes.

Kale - Lacinato Microgreens: antioxidants, fiber, Vitamins A, C, and K, iron, and copper

Lettuce Leaf - Lollo Rosso Microgreens: Vitamins B, C, and K, folic acid, and fiber

www.trueleafmarket.com (heirloom, non-G.M.O., organic seeds)

Elk from my sister's home in the pristine Colorado mountain wilderness: wildcrafted!

WILDCRAFT

verb | ˈwīldkraft |

gather herbs, plants, and fungi from the wild

As I learned more and more about nutrition, I realized there are so many modern obstacles for finding nutrients! I started thinking about the diets of the animals I was eating. At first I thought hunting "wild" animals was the answer. I imagined the animals roaming in my area free of feed lots and antibiotics, but then I remembered that they would have access to the G.M.O. corn fields sprayed with chemicals. I realized that I would need to find farmers who farm naturally (the most "wild" option). The eatwild.com website provides such a valuable service by creating a directory to help people find grass-fed animals. Even when I find a farm, I ask many, many questions! Some consider themselves natural and 100% grass-fed but then feed grain or corn to catch the animals.

I am always hunting for wildcrafted food, clothing, and shelter ingredients.

FOOD FINDING RESOURCES

Grass-fed BEEF from local Minnesota and Wisconsin farmers WWW.EATWILD.COM (steaks, tenderloin, roasts, ground, liver, bones for broth, bone marrow, back ribs, tongue, cheek, kidney, fat for rendering)

Grass-fed BISON from WWW.NORTHSTARBISON.COM (bone broth, bone marrow, ground, liver, glands, heart, fat for rendering)

Wild-caught whole SALMON from WWW.LOKIFISH.COM (whole salmon, salmon roe)

Wild-caught brown SHRIMP from WWW.USWELLNESS.COM

Grass-fed LAMB from local Wisconsin farmers WWW.EATWILD.COM or WWW.MILLERSORGANIC-FARM.COM or WWW.NORTHSTARBISON.COM (ground, ribs, leg-of-lamb, kidney, liver, bones for broth, fat for rendering)

Dried ANCHOVIES from WWW.RADIANTLIFECATALOG.COM

California OLIVE OIL from WWW.RADIANTLIFECATALOG.COM

Traditionally-made COCONUT OIL from WWW.TROPICALTRADITIONS.COM (gallons, coconut cream small jars)

Weston Price Shopping Guide-recommended Organic AVOCADO OIL from WWW.MOUNTAINROSEHERB.COM

HIMALAYAN SALT from WWW.HIMALAYANCRYSTALSALT.COM

BAJA GOLD SEA SALT from WWW.BAJAGOLDSEASALT.COM

Cucumbers, leafy greens, herbs, lemons/limes from ST PAUL FARMER'S MARKET, RIVER MARKET, FRESH & NATURAL, MISSISSIPPI MARKET, yard garden!

Whole food SUPPLEMENTS from WWW.RADIANTLIFECATALOG.COM (cod liver oil, skate oil, emu oil, alma tablets, turmeric capsules, liquid mineral drops for remineralizing filtered water, sink and shower water filters)

AZOMITE POWDER (DIRT!) from WWW.TRUELEAFMARKET.COM

Resources I use to find all food:
WWW.EATWILD.COM
WESTON PRICE SHOPPING GUIDE
WWW. LOCALHARVEST.ORG

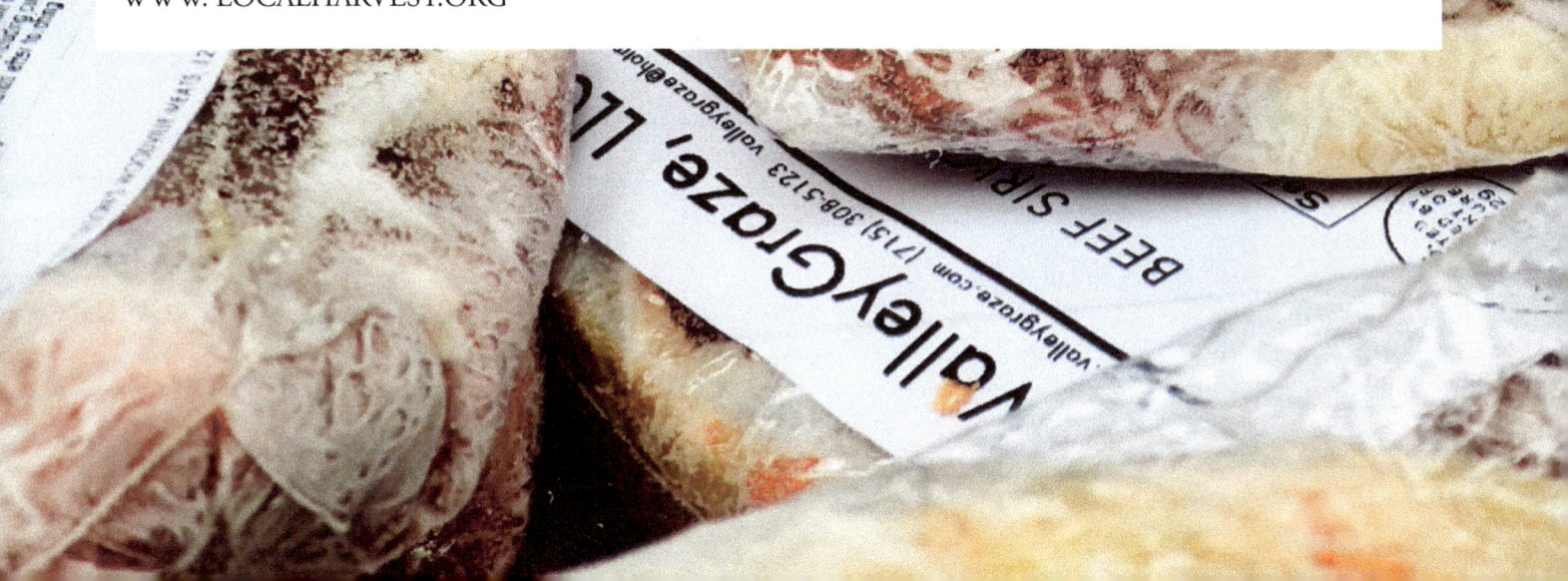

COOKING

1. find the absolute purest, most impeccable ingredients (considering soil, plant, and animal health)

2. prepare ingredients simply (removing from freezer, thawing if necessary, adding salt and massaging organic real oil into its surface to marinate for 1 hour or 1+ days), always eat/cook food at room temperature, eat raw or cook LOW and SLOW 150 degrees overnight, reheat for an hour at 150 degrees, use traditional toxin-free cookware and real fat (A LOT of fat), reuse fat and cooking juices as dressings or dips or for more cooking

3. use all senses (listening for sizzling; smelling aromas during heating; looking, touching, and tasting)

4. make bone broth often for freezing and for consuming daily

5. have learned that the best flavor is in the cooking juices, little bits, and fat

6. have learned that salt and fat are secret-ingredient weapons (I search for the best of both)

7. heat is a tool! sometimes I use the top of a warm oven when I want to apply really gentle heat; sometimes I use the heat from a cooling pan to delicately wilt leafy greens or herbs

What I did: I remember seeing the movie <u>Julia & Julie</u> in the theater and deciding I wanted to learn how to cook! After reading several books from the library I remember calling my mom on the phone crying, "Mom! Do I have to make broth from scratch?!" and she replied, "No one makes broth from scratch! They sell it in one of the aisles at the co-op...broth-in-a-box!"

KITCHEN TIPS I USE RELIGIOUSLY

1. When shopping, choosing heavy-for-their-size lemons and limes.

2. Rolling lemons and limes on the countertop before using (using arm muscle to break apart the inside to release more juice).

3. Revering the fragility/rancidity of oils (storing in cool, dark places without light exposure; opening bottle only when necessary and not very often; keeping oil/butters contaminate-free by keeping fingers out of it and using a clean wooden spatula to extract).

4. Allowing foods to come to room temperature before cooking and/or consuming.

5. Using olive oil as a substitute for pepper (impeccable, traditionally-made pepper is impossible to find!).

6. Using A LOT of fat! For cooking, for eating, for EVERYTHING!

7. Cooking "low and slow" using temperatures 150 or 225 degrees for everything; never over medium on stovetop even "deep frying" in the wok.

8. Placing a magnetic strip tool holder above the stove for 2 knives, a scissors, and a fork tong.

9. Marinating, marinating, marinating (Himalayan sea salt + highest quality olive oil, salt and then massaging oil into meat and waiting, waiting, waiting 1 hour - days).

10. Using the best salt I can find to enhance flavor (for everything!). I use diffent kinds from different regions.

11. Finding the absolute BEST ingredients I can find for everything! (purest, most natural, most pristine, most impeccable) then doing my BEST to keep those ingredients pure (only adding the best salt and the best fat)!

12. In addition, keeping cookware free from any contaminating substances (only wiping with lemons or herbs).

13. Knowing the secret of sauces: the leftover pan juice, tiny bits, and fat! That's it!

14. Place steak in a preheated pan (sizzling) and don't move it until it has been seared (beautiful brown crust).

15. Using residual heat as a tool. Sometimes I place a pan on top of a heating oven so that it gets just a bit of heat. Sometimes I add herbs or leafy greens to a cooling pan so they wilt slightly.

16. Practice, practice, practice! I remember reading that gaining cooking skills takes practice; I was so disappointed! I was hoping to learn through the books and have immediate success! Now after several years of cooking (practice!), I have gained the skills I was so anxious to have.

I remember reading from several different sources that many chefs consider the surface of their cookware for flavors thus the use of soaps and chemicals is not recommended. I also remember reading that chemicals can take away from our nutrition and health. I remember feeling certain that I did not want to work against myself since I was exerting so much time, energy, and expense in finding, eating, and preparing impeccable nutrient-dense food; I started to use lemons and limes as "cleaners" for all of my unglazed, natural-materials clay cookware. I squeeze some juice and use the cut citrus fruit to scrub: toxin-free, naturally antiseptic, and adding delicious future flavor! If I ever need abrasion beyond the citrus rind I use sea salt. H E L L O !   H A P P I N E S S

"According to some writers, earthenware reveals the 'gout du terroir,' which means a 'taste of the earth' in French" (mymoroccanfood.com).

Care for unglazed clay cookware: use heat diffusers; start with very low heat or a cold oven and turn up heat gently after cooking; place on a wooden board to prevent thermal shock/cracking

WEEKLY FEEDING for HAPPY DOGS

5-6 days/week (1-2 days fasting)

each day: raw meaty bones and muscle (always served together)

once a week: liver

once a week: offal

1-2 times/week: raw green tripe (as the meal)

1-2 times/month: whole oily fish

whenever available: bone broth

whenever available: fur, table scraps (some fruit/vegetable peelings liquidized for better digestability)

TIPS

No cooked bones EVER

Supervise recreational bones

Feed puppies as much as they want

Feed liver 5%

Feed other organs 5-10%

Supplement oily fish if using grain-fed meat

Fresh water

Farm animal bones = too large!

Less broken teeth when bones have meat

Weight watch: feel ribs but not see ribs

Feed roughly 2-3% body weight daily

Feed roughly 15-20% body weight weekly

Feed meat and bone as one large piece

Ripping large piece = happy dogs w/clean teeth

Feed once a day

Fast 1-2 days/week

RAW FOOD for HAPPY DOGS

RAW MEATY BONES (RMB) 40%
small dogs (whole quail, chicken wings 30% of meal and 70% meat, duck feet, chicken necks, cornish hen)
medium dogs (all the small dog bones, chicken backs 35%, duck necks, chicken quarters, pork tails, duck wings)
large dogs (whole prey rabbit, turkey neck, lamb head, pork feet, turkey feet, whole chicken, lamb necks 50%, pork necks 30%, turkey necks 50%, ox tails, beef ribs 30%, turkey tails)
any meaty bone that can be completely consumed by your dog!
keep phosophorus and calcium ratio 1:1 over time
phosphorus = meat
calcium = bone
some things are bonier than others (adjust 30%/50%)

BONE CONTENT
chicken (leg quarters 30%, split breast 20%, thigh 15%, drumstick 30%, wing 45%, neck 36%, back 45%, feet 60%, head 75%)
beef (ribs 52%, oxtails 45-65%)
lamb (ribs 27%, shoulder blade 24%, whole shoulder arm and blade 21%)
duck (whole 28%, neck 50%, feet 60%)
turkey (whole turkey 21%, thigh 21%, drumstick 20%, wing 37%, neck 42%, back 41%)
rabbit (whole rabbit including fur 10%, whole dressed 28%)

OFFAL (10-15% OR 1-2 MEALS/WEEK)
fries (testicles), head meat (cheek and jowl), heart, kidney, lips, liver, melt (spleen), rinds (skin), sweetbreads (thymus gland or pancreas), tail, tongue
if loose stools try feeding small amounts each day

RAW GREEN TRIPE (2 OR MORE MEALS/WEEK)
perfect balance of calcium to phosphorus (1:1)
rich in digestive enzymes and Lactobacillus Acidophilus, vitamin B
contains the essential fatty acids, Linoleic and Linolenic in the proper ratio
(tripe from grass-fed animals)

RECREATIONAL BONES
beef neck bones
*SUPERVISE
(use later for pet bone broth)

CALCIUM SUPPLEMENT
blend eggshells (pastured) until powdery
use 1/2 tsp/lb of meat

BISON TRIPE

NOT FOR HUMAN CONSUMPTION

NORTHSTAR BISON, LLC
RICE LAKE, WI 54868

CLOTHING

As my research about nutrition expanded, I learned from several different sources that our skin absorbs much of what is put on it (like administered drugs through transdermal patches) and should be considered as much as what we put in our mouths!

About this same time I learned that around 75% of the world's pesticide use is for cotton. I thought why would I spend this much time, money, and energy finding impeccably pure and nutritious food to eat if what I am putting on my skin (my largest organ) is causing harm to my body!?

So the next stage of my healthy (and happiest!) life began: the search for "nutritious" clothing and skin products.

What a transformation! I never expected the joy that would follow such an overwhelming undertaking!

"We've all heard the question, 'what are you wearing?' Most likely you've never answered, 'petroleum, pesticides, perfluorochemicals, and antimony, with cadmium accessories.' Yet in most cases, that would be the honest answer... The development of man-made material has necessitated the invention of thousands of new chemicals... the chemicals, which now have direct contact with our bodies, can be absorbed through the skin... in a way, our clothes have become as highly processed as our food; both have moved from healthy and natural to convenient and toxic."

- Dr Myron Wentz & Dave Wentz

"Buy less, choose well, make it last...we are moving from a culture of appearances to a culture of values, and everything we do, wear and eat will reflect that." - Johanna Björk

Finding nutritious clothing is similar to finding nutritious food: the proof is in the process. If a farmer or producer is creating an impeccable product, then the process will be described in every meticulous detail. I now know that it is necessary to visit the farm (or speak directly through phone or email) and ask questions. Many "natural" food and clothing products are not at all natural after asking questions. Many times if a website does not include the impeccable details in its descriptions, I have learned it is almost always a waste of my time to call, chat or email.

One of my biggest challenges in this endeavor has been color! It is so rare to find companies producing textiles using natural plant dyes or colorgrown fibers.

One of the most unexpected outcomes of this often times discouraging journey has been the utmost joy I receive from treating my life and health impeccably! Every time I touch or put on my natural clothing, I feel infinitely happy for doing everything possible to protect my health. Natural clothing smells neutral rather than chemical, is extremely comfortable, breathable, soft and beautiful!

I also unexpectedly found endless joy from choosing my clothing items with purpose and the fulfillment that follows.

I found immense joy and freedom from having only a few, necessary, well-crafted clothing items. My impeccably clean clothing and shoes are expensive and sometimes custom made. I have learned to choose wisely and to consider how a new item will fit with the other items. I found great comraderie and joy in discovering through Jennifer L Scott's *Madame Chic* books that the French have always done this naturally with what she terms the "ten-item wardrobe." The surprising result is a timeless, "delicious," durable, divinely beautiful, colors-of-nature, nutritious wardrobe! H E L L O !   H A P P I N E S S

"Toxic color comes at an enormous environmental and human cost. Many do not realize that although we do not eat our clothing and textiles, the same materials that go into making our garments and disposing of them become us. Residue from synthetic chemicals used to make dyes can be found in our air, water, and soil... [from a New York Times article] Dan Fagin details, our current methods of devouring fast fashion and synthetic dyes have us in 'A Cancer Cycle From Here to China.'"

- Sasha Duerr, founder of Permacouture Institute

"Every time you spend money, you're casting a vote for the kind of world you want." - Anne Lappé

WHAT I WEAR

Majority of wardrobe from WWW.GAIACONCEPTIONS.COM (organic cotton, wool, velour, thermal, linen, silk, natural dyes, skirts/shirts/dresses/pants/shorts/leggings)

Significant amount from WWW.INDUSTRYOFALLNATIONS.COM (organic cotton and denim, natural dyes, shirts/t-shirts/sweatershirts/sweaters/denim jacket)

Undergarments from WWW.FAERIESDANCE.COM (organic cotton lingerie/sleepwear)

Undergarments from WWW.COTTONIQUE.COM (undergarments)

Some pieces from WWW.RAWGANIQUE.COM (organic cotton, fleece, denim, linen jackets/socks/fleece pants/fleece jacket)

Some pieces from WWW.ETSY.COM (organic cotton, wool, linen, knit or crocheted legwarmers/anklewarmers/mittens/hats/scarves/knee-high socks/sweaters/skirts/purse/bikini/halter top/silk kimonos)

Sweaters, bikini top, halter top, mittens, hats, scarves, purse, headband, dog sweater, rug, and dog leash from LEARNING HOW TO CROCHET & KNIT with organic, toxin-free yarn from WWW.ECOBUTTERFLY.COM, WWW.HANDWEAVERS.COM/YARN, and WWW.ETSY.COM

Many shoes from WWW.SWEDISHHASBEENS.COM (vegetable-tanned leather ankle boots, vegetable-tanned leather sandal heels, vegetable-tanned leather clog heels, vegetable-tanned leather bag)

Several shoes from WWW.SOLUDOS.COM (all jute-soled, natural materials espadrilles)

Several shoes from WWW.PO-ZU.COM (vegetable-tanned leather boots, organic wool ankle boots and shoes, vegetable-tanned suede boots and shoes, coconut-hulled soles)

Multiple pairs from WWW.OLLIWORLD.COM or WWW.PLANETFLOPS.COM (natural-rubber flip-flops)

Waterproof knee-high boots from WWW.LECHAMEAU.COM/US

Vegetable-tanned leather knee-high boots from WWW.BEDSTU.COM

Organic, toxin-free material tennis shoes from WWW.VEJA.COM

Vegetable-tanned leather bag from WWW.SANDLUNDHOSSAIN.COM

Talisman from WWW.PYRRA.COM and pure palladium chain from WWW.SORELLA.COM

VIDEOS AND PINS

YouTube videos of wardrobe and shoes (https://www.youtube.com/channel/UCKXc4jhkNgHnyWG_ZN-U7ONQ)

Vimeo videos of wardrobe and shoes (https://vimeo.com/laurapaulisich)

Pinterest boards of wardrobe and shoes (https://www.pinterest.com/paulisichauthor/)

Or follow links on home page of www.laurapaulisich.com or www.myhappylifeforsale.com

REASONS

"Marc Lappé: Sensitive assays have detected residues of over a hundred different foreign chemicals and metals in our tissues - compounds and substances that were virtually absent from the environments of our predecessors." - Dr Pitcairn

"For many chemicals, there is no information on dermal absorption…Until the beginning of the 20th century, the skin was thought to be completely inert and impermeable to chemicals that might otherwise enter the body. While the skin does act as a barrier, it is not a complete barrier. Many chemicals do penetrate the skin, either intentionally or unintentionally, and cutaneous metabolism does occur. Because of its large surface area, the skin may be a major route of entry into the body in some exposure situations…The transport of chemicals through the skin is a complex process. The skin is a complex organ and also a living membrane. The skin and the environment are in constant interaction…Risk assessment is a process by which the extent of exposure is compared against the hazard (intrinsic toxicity) of the chemical to determine whether it is likely to result in harm to the exposed individual(s). Exposure to a chemical can be by oral, inhalational, or dermal routes; however, in an occupational and many environmental and consumer settings, the latter two are the major routes… Since most laboratory animal testing is by oral administration, but the predominant route of exposure for pesticides, for example, is by skin absorption, the extent of dermal absorption needs to be determined to perform an occupational risk assessment (route-to-route extrapolation)…The skin is not an almost impermeable barrier to chemicals, as was originally thought. Now there are many databases describing skin permeation of chemicals…Determination of dermal absorption is a key element of the risk assessment of pesticides, biocides, cosmetics, pharmaceuticals, and industrial chemicals. The potential exposure can occur during the manufacturing process, transport, and the end use of products. In addition, exposure to chemicals can occur in the environment…dermal absorption has to be considered in scenarios where these neonates are dermally exposed to contaminants present in bath water or to chemicals in hygienic or diaper rash products…It needs to be recognized that emerging technologies such as nanoparticles may have unanticipated toxicological consequences following contact with the skin." - World Health Organization

"Perpetual use of 'big' shoes weaken feet, increase injury risk and increase pain throughout lower extremeties." - Mark Sisson

Once I learned about herbicides in clothing, I stayed away! Just like I stay away from chemicals in food.

After all the energy and perseverance put into building and finding a "nutritious" wardrobe (toxin-free, organic, natural materials, plant dyes, natural dyes) every piece of clothing is a gift that I hold sacred and feel extremely grateful to own, thus I take care of it; love it; use it! My clothes create joy because they have a specific purpose: to keep me safe, protected, warm, and healthy.

"The benefits of the ten-item wardrobe are vast. Your shopping habits will become healthier. You will waste less money; you will not be a slave to consumerism; you won't be tempted by old pulls that used to draw you in (*final sale! clearance! last chance!*). You will clarify your true style and embrace it. You will be forced to wear your nice clothes on a daily basis by getting rid of the ragged or unflattering ones, and therefore you will look presentable always. When you wake up in the morning, the choice of what to wear will be easy because everything in your wardrobe will go with everything else. Poised people look presentable, assert their style, and are comfortable in their clothing. The ten-item wardrobe will get you there." - Jennifer L. Scott

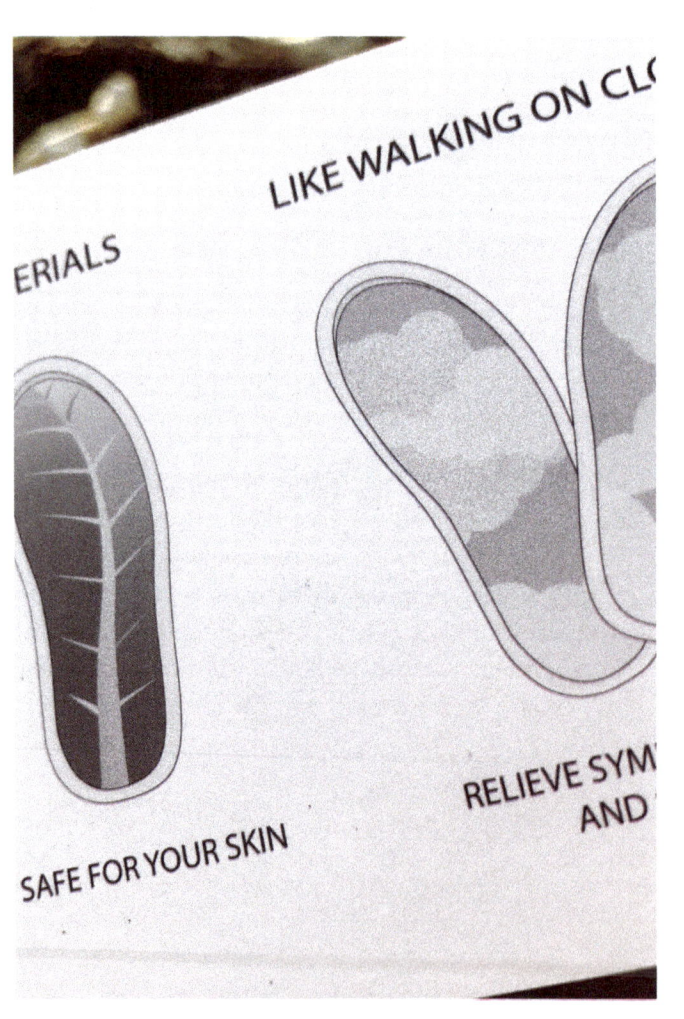

Ayu Neem

Health Benefits*:
Anti bacterial/fungal and anti-septic qualities, relief from eczema
& psoriasis related conditions, dry skin itch

Main Ingredients:
Neem (Azadirachta indica)

Other key herbs /plants used:
Wild-Crafted Accacia Catechu, Wild-Crafted Ficus Glomerata, Ficus religiosa Linn,
Wild-Crafted Garcina Xanthochymus (close relative to Garcinia mangostana) Mallotus Philipincensis

All organic ingredients

*This product is not intended to diagnose, treat or cure any disease.

100% recycled

www.ayuvastra.ie, www.ayuvastra.uk.com

SAFE SOLES

I remember reading that the soles of the feet absorb the most of what they touch. I always think of this when choosing shoes.

I've been searching for safe soles ever since. I've learned about all of the extremely harmful chemicals in leather and learned that the traditional and natural method of tanning leather is to use the animal's brain ("brain-tanned" leather). Obviously, these shoes are impossible to find!

The footbeds I wear include natural and toxin-free rubber (flip-flops), cork, toxin-free wood, vegetable-tanned (chrome-free) leather, toxin-free jute, organic cotton and earth (barefoot).

"We have only scratched the surface, this is something that has to be dealt with. Clothes are worn day and night during our entire life. We must find out if textile chemicals go into our skin and what it means to our health. It is very difficult to assess and requires considerably more research," says Conny Östman, Professor in Analytical Chemistry.
Source: https://www.sciencedaily.com/releases/2015/10/151023084508.htm

1. follow Jennifer L. Scott's ten-item wardrobe suggestions but with toxin-free clothing and shoes

2. find organic cotton, hemp, wool, velour, fleece, thermal, silk, denim fabrics

3. search for and sometimes find textiles colored with natural and plant dyes and colorgrown colors

4. have most clothing custom made by Gaia Conceptions and some custom made by Etsy

5. knit or crochet some clothing using organic cotton or wool yarn

6. interchange all clothing into endless outfits because of harmonious natural colors

7. use all of my clothing and shoes until unwearable and then use the material to make other things (cutoffs, swimwear, pillows, rugs, rags, dog bedding, etc.) (Everything is so valuable to me now: it is impossible to discard! This is such a drastic difference from my previous habit of constantly consuming and discarding.)

What I did: purchased endless "cute" clothing and shoes wasting time, energy, money, and spirit (a relentless cycle of feeling shameful about unused items paired with the insatiable desire for wanting more items). I also felt overwhelmed by keeping track of everything, choosing what to wear, piles of laundry, overstuffed closets, knowing how much I was spending and then bewildered by the fact that I always ended up wearing the same few pieces of clothing over and over!

TALISMAN

noun | tal·is·man | \'ta-les-men , -lez- \

1 : an object held to act as a charm to avert evil and bring good fortune
2 : something producing apparently magical or miraculous effects

Investing in one meaningful, purposeful, real-material talisman has been the best decision. It has changed my life and brought such happiness! Every day I can't wait to put it on and wear it for life. It doesn't take any time to decide what to wear, and it enchances all outfits. Because I researched and thought a lot about what I wanted as a charm, the special meaning of my necklace creates a marked feeling every day. It has earned a place as a necessary belonging in my apartment and life. H E L L O !   H A P P I N E S S

SHELTER

While researching the toxins in cotton and clothing, I accidently read about the harmful toxins in U. S. manufactured mattresses. Like all of the previous learning, once I became aware I had to change.

Similar to finding toxin-free clothing, this started an equally daunting task. I felt like the bed and bedding were the most immediate concerns because of the significant time spent there and the most exposed skin and direct contact.

Next came towels, rugs, car seat coverings, shampoo, toothpaste, deodorant, cleaning supplies until eventually I found alternatives for all household items!

I found more and more joy as purpose, usefulness, and freedom increased.

My walls and space are filled with inspiration: birch bark hearts, photo wall collages and murals, kitchen tool collages, open shelving to display handmade sweaters and shoes, open shelving to display traditionally-made clay cookware and olive wood dishes, crystal and rock wall and floor displays. So easy it is hard to believe it is possible: biodegradable and beautiful; useful and artistic. H E L L O ! H A P P I N E S S

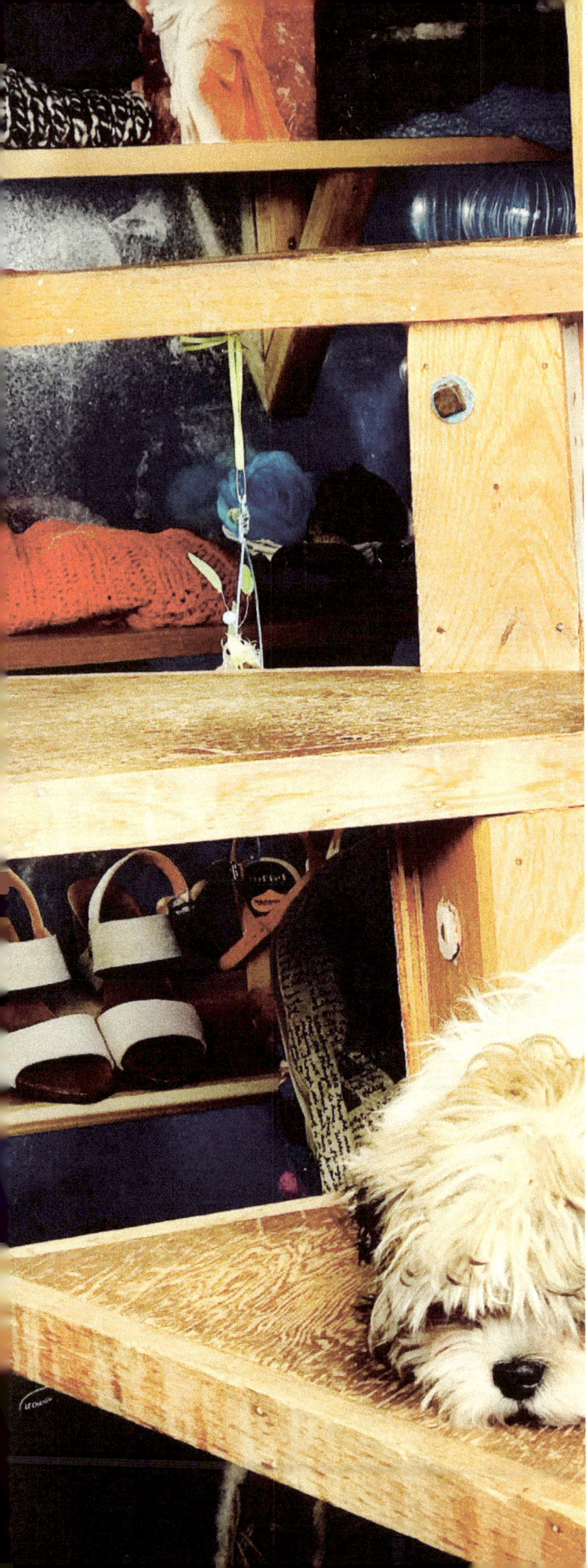

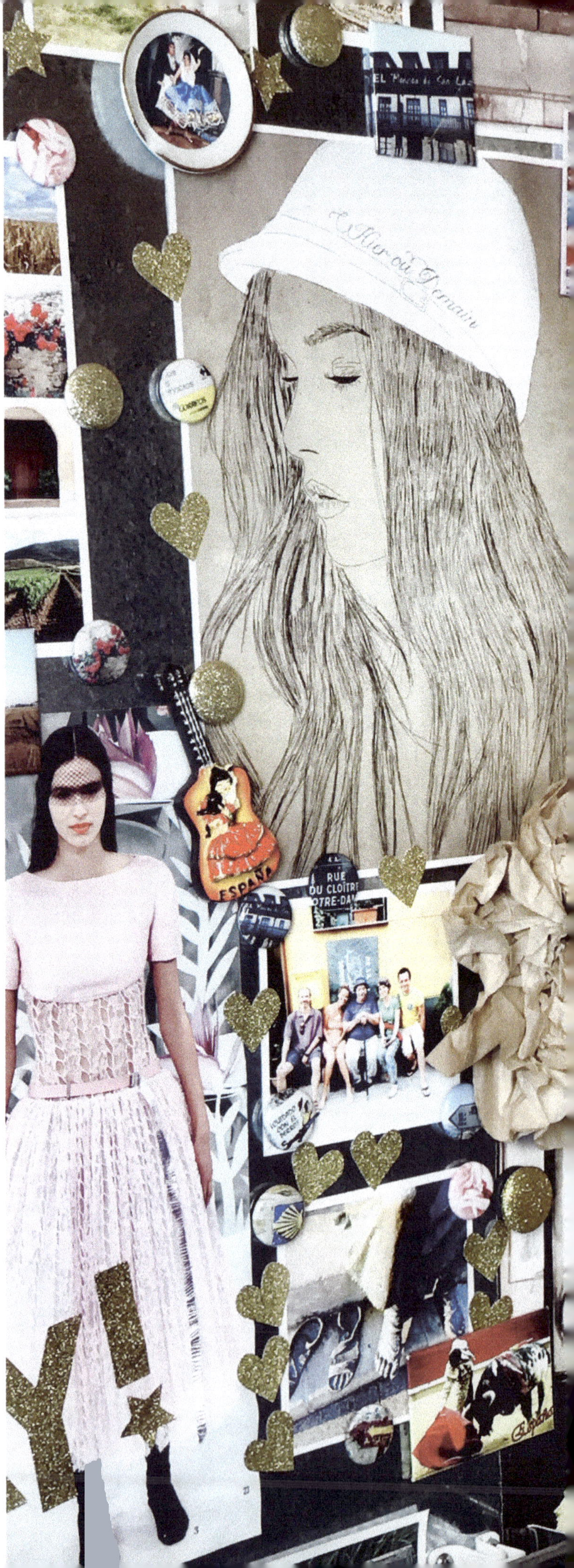
ESPAÑA
RUE
DU CLOITRE

"Our most important ecosystems are our homes and workplaces. They're either making us well or making us sick. Each of us is a cellular being who interacts with every substance we encounter no matter how miniscule it is. What we're after here is true health…making the space in which we live as safe as it's meant to be."
- Dr Myron Wentz & Dave Wentz

OBESOGENS

"...researchers are gathering convincing evidence of chemical 'obesogens'—dietary, pharmaceutical, and industrial compounds that may alter metabolic processes and predispose some people to gain weight. Most known or suspected obesogens are endocrine disruptors. Many are widespread, and exposures are suspected or confirmed to be quite common...In one 2010 study, Kurunthachalam Kannan, a professor of environmental sciences at the University at Albany, State University of New York, documented organotins in a designer handbag, wallpaper, vinyl blinds, tile, and vacuum cleaner dust collected from houses. Phthalates, plasticizers that also have been related to obesity in humans, occur in many PVC items as well as in scented items such as air fresheners, laundry products, and personal care products." - www.ncbi.nlm.nih.gov/pmc/articles/PMC3279464/

I remember reading "the nose knows"(*The Healthy Home*). With all of the endless manmade chemicals entering the environment our senses become immune to them. Just like our powerful and delicate palates, the nose's abilities become compromised around compromising ingredients! The author advises to trust our noses, and if something smells dangerous it is dangerous!

I used to be a "normal" consumer of toxin-filled products and foods. My nose no longer worked. I would walk around stores, malls, schools and hospitals not noticing toxins. Now living free of toxin-filled products and no longer going to stores, if I do enter a store, I gasp for fresh air. I can taste the poisonous fumes. I've become "chemically sensitive"(i.e. my nose works again and it is saying "GET AWAY FROM THE DANGER PLEASE NOW!").

SUCCESSFUL UNDERARM STRATEGY

I was so excited to read in Sally Fallon's book about fat that tea tree oil mixed with coconut oil can be used as deodorant. I loved this idea! I used it for several months but eventually disliked the smell.

After more searching, I tried mixing peppermint oil with almond oil in a small container. I love this method! The aroma and the feel of the oil are delicious!

I also read that Wellness Mama sprays her transdermal therapy magnesium spray on her underarms each night as a deodorant. After several successful months now, my Successful Underarm Strategy is to include the underarms at night when I am spraying magnesium spray for transdermal therapy, then in the morning I rub the peppermint oil mixture under my arms. Every once in a while I will spray a layer of witch hazel. H E L L O ! H A P P I N E S S

TOOTH HEALTH

1. drink daily bone broth
2. eat a nutrient-dense plant and animal diet

TOOTH ENAMEL/FRESH BREATH ROUTINE

1. remineralizing tooth powder (turmeric + activated charcoal + bentonite clay + Celtic sea salt)

2. tooth powder (baking soda + Celtic sea salt + clove oil + peppermint oil + arrowroot powder)

3. Hydrofloss gum cleaner (warm water + sea salt)

4. peppermint drop on tongue (if necessary)

5. organic clove "lozenge" (if necessary)

6. whipped body butter as lip balm

CLEAN CLEANING

lemon cleaner spray (lemon-infused organic vinegar + 20 drops lemon + 20 drops orange essential oils)

liquid soap nuts for laundry, hand soap, dog shampoo (40 soapnuts boiled then simmered 1 hour in 4 cups water + 20 drops lavender oil)

pine toilet cleaner (rosemary & pine needle-infused organic vinegar + pine and rosemary essential oils)

flea and floor powder (food grade diatomaceous earth + dry neem + dry yarrow)

SPECIAL-OCCASION CLEANING

Angel spray (frankincense + myrrh + sandalwood)
carpet freshener (1 cup baking soda + 10-15 drops lavender)
vacuum freshener (add essential oil to vacuum filter or to paper towel pieces and vacuum pieces)
kitchen degreaser (vinegar + baking soda + orange oil + hot water)
goo remover (baking soda + coconut oil + lemon oil = paste and let sit on stickiness)
laundry brightener (squeeze lemon juice into laundry and lemon essential oil)
drawer and slumber satchets (dried lavender buds + lavender oil in small organic bags + rosemary for clothes)
wood and leather cleaner (olive oil + lemon cleaner and wipe clean)
pot and pan scrubber (baking soda in pan then add lemon cleaner to let sit)
potpourri: dried flowers (dehydrater or 150 degree oven + rosemary + lavender oils + flowers)
scented light bulb (drop lavender/peppermint/frankincense/lemon/orange onto lightbulb and turn on)
toilet paper roll freshener (add a few drops of essential oils to the cardboard center)
burn relief (lavender oil)
stubborn stains toilet (borax + pine toilet cleaner + pine + eucalyptus; pour and let sit overnight)
jewelry cleaner (hot water + baking soda + lemon oil; add jewelry; sit several minutes; scrub; rinse; dry)
stovetop cleaner paste (baking soda + lemon cleaner = paste; let sit; rub off)
vinyl floors (hot water + lemon cleaner + borax + peppermint oil; mop)
bee stings (lavender oil directly on sting)
splinter remover (clove oil on splinter and wait several minutes; repeat until begins to dislodge; remove)
toothache (clove oil to tooth and gum)
hand sanitizer (few lemon oil drops on hands; rub hands together)
drawer freshener (organic cotton balls + lavender)
travel bed bug spray (cedarwood oil + distilled water and spray)
bug spray (distilled water + witch hazel + tea tree + lavender + rosemary oils)
dog accident (soak up then add lemon cleaner + baking soda to bubble; blot clean and vacuum)
lemongrass linen spray (lemongrass oil + distilled water)
dust mite bed cleaner (baking soda + lavender + tea tree oils; sprinkle on mattress/pillows; let sit hours; vacuum)

Homemade heart-shaped wire trivet

WHAT'S IN MY(toxin-free)BAG?

handmade roller ball perfume

essential oil as perfume

organic clove "lozenges" for fresh breath

peppermint essential oil for emergency fresh breath (ONE drop on tongue in emergencies)

handmade body butter lip balm

lemon essential oil as hand sanitizer

current Weston Price Shopping Guide

small (enriching) book (5" x 5" *Essential Oils* or *Four Agreements* or *Fail, Fail Better*)

homemade small biodegradable ideabook

toxin-free tissues

sometimes toxin-free yarn and toxin-free wooden knitting needles

organic cotton shopping tote

Indian ink pens (different tips)

Raw Cedarwood pencils

sometimes raw wood colored pencils

sometimes *Wise Traditions* magazine

sometimes *Dogs Naturally* magazine

Note: use most of the items daily, some weekly and a few rarely

What used to be in my bag: cute container tissues, cute label hand sanitizer, cute container mints, more cute container mints, smaller cute handbags and pouches, cute container mirror, cute container lip balm, more cute container lip balm, another cute container lip balm, cute notepad, cute pen, two or three pairs of cute sunglasses, cute container first aid kit, cute container travel kit, Lucky (shopping) magazine, Anthropologie (shopping) catalog, checkbook, two or three cute wallets (couldn't ever decide), cute socks, cute containers of lotion and powder and perfume, sometimes cute shoes, cute kitschy objects, cute sweater, cute travel photo album, cute book. Note: I rarely used anything in the bag!

LP No 17 (oil perfume)

homemade, unique scent using the purest essential oils from AHAherb.com (giving away all my secrets!)

top notes (5-20%):	middle notes (50-80%):	base notes (5-20%):
peppermint	rose	sandalwood
lemon	rosemary	frankincense
lavender	geranium	myrrh
eucalyptus	chamomile	rose absolute
lemongrass	clary sage	cedarwood

I use the large Infinity Jar roller ball for home use and the smallest Infinity Jar roller ball for purse use.

add 80-85 drops of perfume blend
4 ounce jar organic jojoba oil
shake well

LP No 17 ("neat")

apply 1 drop of essential oil undiluted directly on pulse points (wrists, elbows, behind earlobes, temples, neck, underarms, cleavage/sternum, behind knees, ankles) - *Making Love Potions* by S Tourles

FACE CREAM/BODY BUTTER

whipped organic culinary shea butter + olive oil (or argan oil), frankincense/myhrr/rose, orange oil, alcohol-free vanilla extract; use a wooden spatula to remove from large face cream Infinity Jar (no fingers!)

DEODORANT

peppermint oil + avocado oil (at night I spray some of the magnesium spray on my underarms - *Wellness Mama*)

EYELASH/EYEBROW SERUM

castor oil + emu oil + coconut oil + (optional lavender) - *Wellness Mama*

LAVENDER FLOWER BODY POWDER

dried lavender flower powder + lavender and frankincense oils + baking soda + arrowroot powder - *Making Love Potions* by S Tourles

REASONS

"Daily showers may damage the outermost protective layer of the skin and disrupt the delicate balance maintained by the bacterial ecosystem that inhabits our skin...One ammonia-oxidizing bacterium (AOB) is often found in dirt and untreated water, but was once also present in our skin bacteria, before we started washing it away. Scientists believe this bacteria actually kept us clean and fresh-smelling, boosted our immune system, and tamped down inflammation, all by feeding on the ammonia in our sweat and converting it into nitrite and nitric oxide." - Dr Josh Axe

"Go on a short walk in the woods, and take many deep breaths, consciously bringing the scent of the trees into your lungs. This form of aromatherapy is a practice called 'shinrin-yoku,' or 'forest bathing,' in Japanese. Researchers there have found breathing in the antimicrobial organic compounds called phytoncides - the woods' essential oils - decreased cortisol levels and blood pressure, enhanced immune system function, and stabilized nervous system activity." - Dr Josh Axe

"Remember, it's not only what we eat but also what we touch. Everything we press, tap, rub, or nudge sheds microbes or other molecules that are quickly absorbed through our pores and directly into the bloodstream. Our body's largest organ, the skin, is the first line of defense for our immune system - which leaves it vulnerable to the chemical onslaught as well...soap, deodorant, toothpaste, shampoo, hair conditioner, lip balm, sunscreen, body lotion, shaving products...makeup...dishwasher detergent, laundry detergent, floor cleaner, furniture polish, glass cleaner...your goal should be to minimize your exposure to potentially harmful toxins that are proven to not only damage your gut lining and create antibiotic resistance, but affect your body's endocrine system, leaving your thyroid, pancreas, and adrenal glands even more vulnerable than before." - Dr Josh Axe

"Marc Lappé: Sensitive assays have detected residues of over a hundred different foreign chemicals and metals in our tissues - compounds and substances that were virtually absent from the environments of our predecessors." - Dr Pitcairn

"Indoor air pollution is one of the top health risks today. It's due to the fact that so many synthetic substances are now used in the construction of our homes, and there are so many toxins in the products we employ. Combined with the lack of air circulation in many homes, indoor air, is usually much more polluted than outdoor air." - Dr Myron Wentz & Dave Wentz

tea tree oil: "327 medical studies to date proving its benefits as a gentle topical antimicrobial. A little tea tree oil mixed with water or coconut oil is a much safer hand sanitizer than the bottles of brightly colored gel you'll find at the drugstore." - Dr Josh Axe

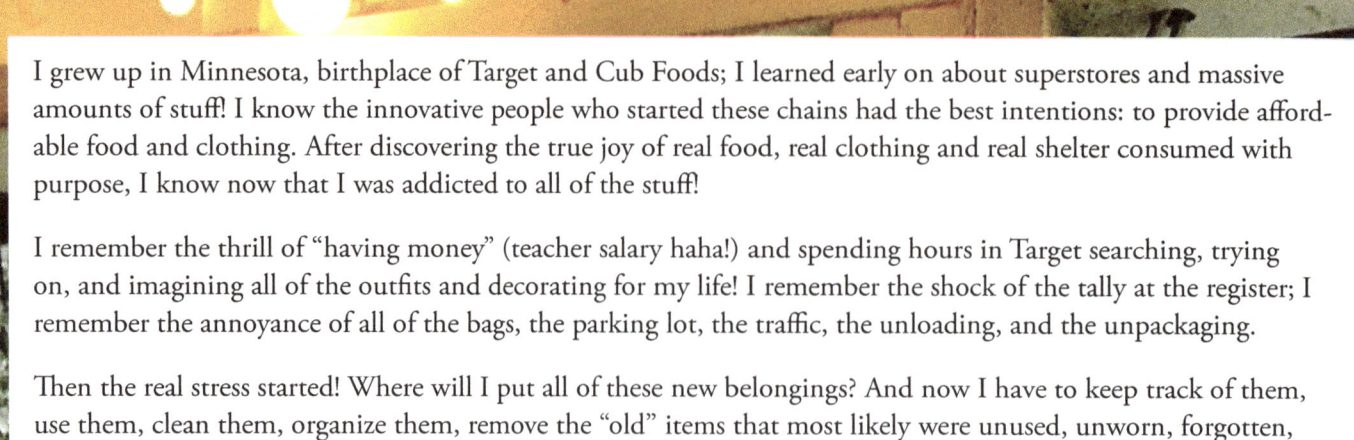

I grew up in Minnesota, birthplace of Target and Cub Foods; I learned early on about superstores and massive amounts of stuff! I know the innovative people who started these chains had the best intentions: to provide affordable food and clothing. After discovering the true joy of real food, real clothing and real shelter consumed with purpose, I know now that I was addicted to all of the stuff!

I remember the thrill of "having money" (teacher salary haha!) and spending hours in Target searching, trying on, and imagining all of the outfits and decorating for my life! I remember the shock of the tally at the register; I remember the annoyance of all of the bags, the parking lot, the traffic, the unloading, and the unpackaging.

Then the real stress started! Where will I put all of these new belongings? And now I have to keep track of them, use them, clean them, organize them, remove the "old" items that most likely were unused, unworn, forgotten, difficult-to-find-among-all-the-other-items.

Then came the stress of remorse. The shame and guilt of consuming-without-use-and-ultimately-discarding not to mention the wastefulness of the money to purchase all of it.

I didn't realize the addictive, maddening, and ultimately extremely depressing cycle I was living until I found real food, real clothing, and real shelter.

Once I was eating with purpose, wearing with purpose and finding shelter with purpose, I experienced and still experience soaring and seemingly limitless daily J O Y !

CTIVE PROPERTIES AND FEATURES A SECURITY SQUARE MP

$$\frac{79\text{-}57}{759}324$$

DATE 6 Oct 20

aze LLC. $ 2

n hundred forty-eight

INVESTMENTS

Freezer $600

Whole beef $2748

Natural rubber knee-high boots $489

Natural rubber queen mattress $1250

Organic heirloom bedding $1628

Brain-tanned buffalo blanket or rug $1,000

Life without shopping: P R I C E L E S S

REASONS

"Liberation from the need to possess. And liberation from conforming to a society built on consumerism. This is the promise of minimalism: to rejoice at the sight of all the things we do not need. And to have our lives finally freed to pursue the things we want to do." - Joshua Becker

"'Do not trouble yourself much to get new things,' Thoreau instructs us. 'Sell your clothes and keep your thoughts.' To be free from the distractions of modern life — of the endlessly diverting display of the ordinary, social world of stuff, stuff and more stuff — allowed a person to focus and think. What could we think if worldly possessions didn't occupy our thoughts? What and whom could we attend to if we stopped attending only to ourselves? Thoreau is often portrayed as a hermit, a lonely individual who rejected all forms of community. He was, in truth, happy enough to abandon the formalities and luxuries of conventional life, but only in an attempt to participate in a wider natural and social order." - John Kaag and Clancy Martin, *The Stone* https://www.nytimes.com/2017/07/10/opinion/thoreaus-invisible-neighbors-at-walden.html

"Richard Foster's principles for simplicity: Buy things for their usefulness rather than their status or prestige. Learn the difference between a real need and an addiction. Develop a habit of giving things away. Avoid unnecessary and short-lived technological gadgets that promise to "save time." Enjoy things without owning them (public libraries and state parks). Nurture awe and appreciation for nature. Spend more time outdoors! Get out -and stay out- of debt. Use plain, honest speech. Say what you mean and keep your commitments. Reject anything that oppresses others (buy Fair Trade products). Live simply so that others may simply live." - Richard Rohr

"Subtracting unneeded stuff multiplies opportunities to pursue things you care about. The result is exponential growth in personal satisfaction. Maybe the life you've always wanted is buried under everything you own!" - Joshua Becker

"There are tons of things in your home and life that you don't use, need, or even particularly want. They just came into your life as impulsive flotsam and jetsam and never found a good exit. Whether you're aware of it or not, this clutter creates indecision and distractions, consuming attention and making unfettered happiness a real chore. It is impossible to realize how distracting all the crap is - whether porcelain dolls, sports cars, or ragged t-shirts - until you get rid of it." - Timothy Ferris

"Are you happy wearing clothes that don't give you pleasure? Do you feel joy when surrounded by piles of unread books that don't touch your heart? Do you think that owning accessories you know you'll never use will ever bring you happiness? Imagine living in a space that contains only things that spark joy. Isn't this the lifestyle you dream of? Keep only those things that speak to your heart. Then take the plunge and discard all the rest. By doing this, you can reset your life and embark on a new lifestyle." - Marie Kondo

"Have nothing in your house that you do not know to be useful, or believe to be beautiful." - William Morris

"When you've finished putting your house in order, your life will change dramatically. Once you have experienced what it's like to have a truly ordered house, you'll feel your whole world brighten." - Marie Kondo

"Surroundings should relate to who you are, what you love, and to what you deem important in life." - George Lois

"In France, there is not an obsession with what is called 'the new materialism.' They are not a society that constantly consumes - going on shopping binges, looking for the next gadget, the next upgrade, the latest *thing* (which accounts for why their homes are so enviably clutter-free). They spend their money on the things that were important to them - high quality food...well-made clothing...To live well - to live within your means and to avoid the seduction of the material world - that is what I call prospering." - Jennifer L. Scott

BELOVED BELONGINGS

scissors
clay cookware ("Black Clay, La Chamba Cookware is well-known throughout Columbia...its origins can be traced back at least 700 years to vases and pitchers found in pre-Columbian archaeological sites. It is still made in the traditional manner by families in a small village on the banks of the Magdalena River in Central Columbia... because the pieces are unglazed, they are completely natural and safe and contain no toxins or lead" - Ancient Cookware)
iron steak pan ("forged iron pan made in Germany by expert blacksmiths since 1857...retains heat...cooks food evenly...lasts forever-it really can...never wash with soap...considered a piece of art by the metal craftsman who works it, and every pan comes out a unique item" - Kaufmann Mercantile)
glass teapot
glass water bottle
homemade heart-shaped wire trivet
brain-tanned buffalo rug ("Totally natural...Tanning can be very toxic. Most buffalo robes are tanned with synthetic tanning agents, formaldehyde or trivalent chrome, even by tanneries who call their product 'eco-friendly.' Then the skins are soaked in miticides and bactericides...we use totally natural tanning agents" - Braintan.com)
Peruvian blanket ("The artisan women of the Andes handspin their sheeps' wool, then dye and treat the wool with natural and organic materials from the earth. These special textiles are uniquely handwoven with traditional Andean techniques and motifs that have been around for centuries...safe from any chemicals...flame-retardant... excellent insulating qualities...natural anti-allergenic material...will last for centuries" - Etsy.com)
organic silk pillowcase ("made from luxurious 19 momme, 100% natural, undyed, chemical free, mulberry silk... contains natural proteins and 18 essential amino acids...a natural heat regulator-keeps you cool when its hot and warm when its cool...naturally hypoallergenic-it does not attract dust mites allowing you to sleep peacefully and allergy free...the easiest thing you can do to prevent aging" - Sleep 'N Beauty)
DIY natural millet hull pillows ("Millet hulls are the shell of the edible seed...grown from organic millet fields in Colorado. The hulls are hypo-allergenic, are not habitable to dust mites, are cool to sleep on and are supportive and durable" - DIY Natural Bedding)
organic natural latex slab mattress ("GOLS organic, durable, sustainable, flexible, hypoallergenic, antimicrobial, dust mite resistant, excellent airflow compared to other foams...call it what you want: 100% all natural, organic, botanical, vegan latex, these latex slabs are as pure as it gets" - DIY Natural Bedding)
colorgrown organic French linen bottom sheet ("heritage organic linen sheets...natural, undyed and unbleached...made by Rawganique from start to finish in Europe for true purity" - Rawganique)
wool comforter ("warm but not hot...the composition and shape of wool's fiber make it free of static and competent at wicking away moisture, regulating your temperature yet insulating you with your own body heat. Our local woolen mill sews it from wool batts from our local farms. The virgin wool is not superwashed, leaving it soft and supple instead of itchy and scratchy" - DIY Natural Bedding)
colorgrown cotton duvet
Hydrofloss
shower brush
colorgrown organic Irish linen towel ("chemical-free, heritage, unbleached and undyed" - Rawganique)

CONSUMABLES

essential oils: lavender, peppermint, lemon, frankincense, rose, sandalwood
DIY beauty products: rollerball perfume oil, lavender flower powder, peppermint oil deodorant, magnesium spray, whipped body butter, toothpowders)
DIY cleaning products: lemon cleaner, laundry soapnuts soap
supplies: biodegradable envelopes, toxin-free paper, biodegradable tape (Ecoenclose), Indian ink pens, cedar wood pencils, biodegradable washi tape

belongingless

nothing to remember

nothing to buy

nothing to clean

nothing to keep

EVERYTHING TO ENJOY!

what i do...

1. decorate with useful belongings (kitchen tools, cookware, sweaters, shoes)

2. decorate with nature! (rocks, stacked rocks, birch bark, crystals, drying flowers)

3. decorate with wall collages (photos, tools, magnets)

4. decorate with open shelving (sweaters, shoes, cookware, tools, yarn)

5. decorate with buffalo rugs and sheepskins (used as bedding and as covers for pillow cushions)

6. decorate walls with paper flowers made from toxin-free tissue

7. use Infinity Jars for all homemade household products using biodegradable tape and Indian ink pens to write labels

What I did: decorated with hundreds of books, unused kitchen appliances, furniture in every room (overextended with a home equity loan), lamps, tables, hundreds of textiles always changing based on "cuteness" (kitchen towels, washclothes, hand towels, bath towels, beach towels, sheets, pillowcases, blankets, blankets, blankets), bags, baskets, CDs, DVDs, wall hangings, calendars, desks...all justified as "necessities!"

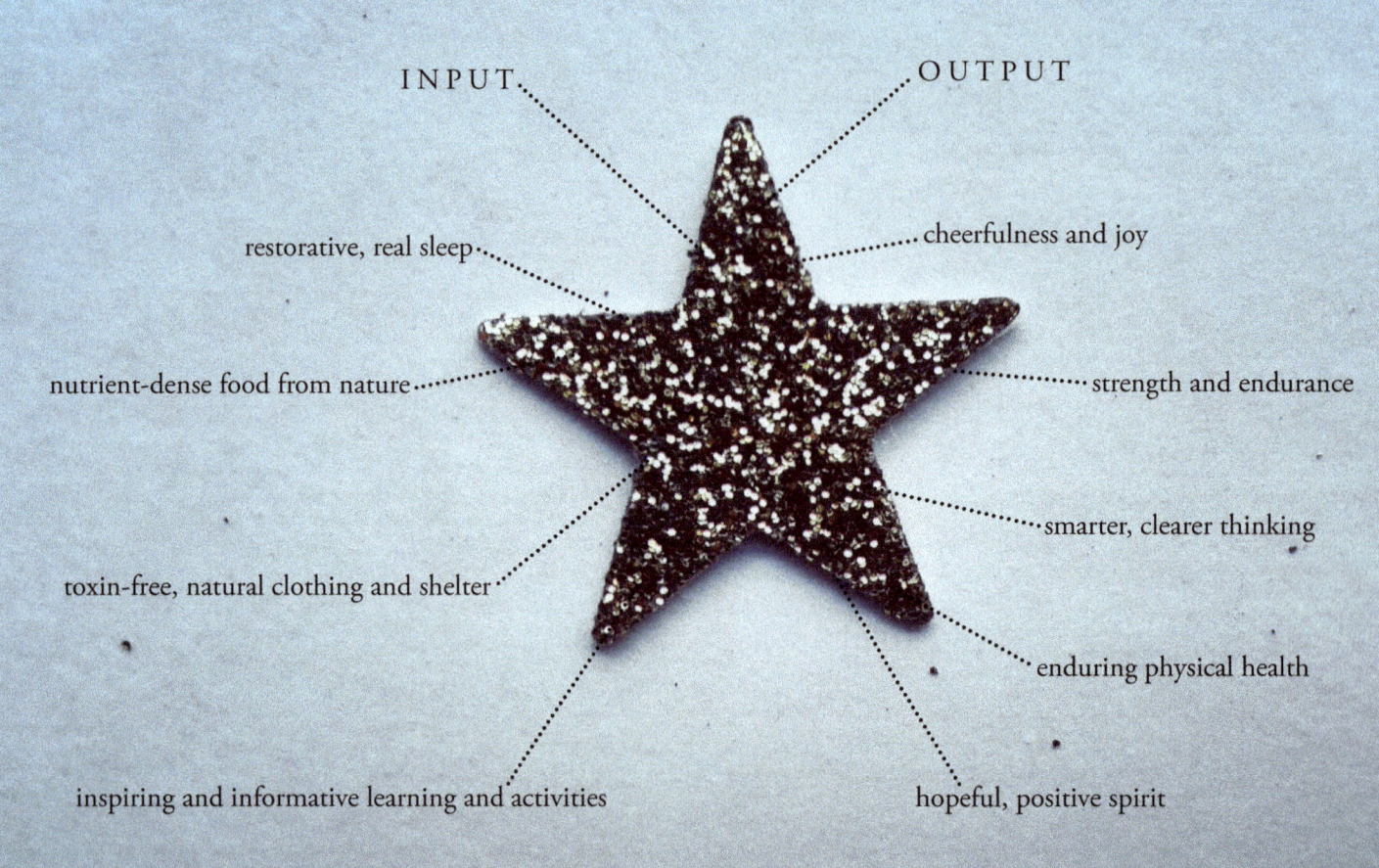

INPUT IMPECCABLE INGREDIENTS

OUTPUT IMPECCABLE HEALTH AND HAPPINESS

SPIRIT

Once I realized "there are no problems," life changed forever! This took a lot of studying, practicing, and retraining of the brain. The practice became habit and then the habit became nature. The most helpful practices have been recognizing stress and then questioning my thinking; practicing and practicing gratitude; acting kind even if not feeling kind; accepting that everything is exactly how it should be; knowing all is well all the time; not taking things personally; participating in positive communities; partnering for accountability; doing service; acting with faith even if not feeling faith; knowing without a doubt that I am responsible for my health and happiness.

There are no words for the impact this has on life except H E L L O ! H A P P I N E S S

CULTIVATING HAPPINESS

Does this amount of sleep enrich my life?
Does this food enrich my life?
Do these clothes enrich my life?
Does this household item enrich my life?
Does this relationship enrich my life?
Does this thought enrich my life?
Does this book enrich my life?
Does this program enrich my life?
Does this activity enrich my life?
Does this use of time enrich my life?

what i do...

1. READ as much as possible! Reading for me is the ultimate way to input inspiring to output inspiring!
2. STUDY the most inspiring reading in order to retrain my brain for the positive
3. PRACTICE gratitude (noticing everything I am grateful for; listing everything I am grateful for; communicating when I am grateful for something; find gratitude even if not feeling grateful)
4. PRACTICE living one moment at a time (noticing when I start thinking about other things during activities like eating, driving, talking with someone...the more I practice this the faster I can recognize it and return to the moment)
5. PRACTICE separating myself from brain chatter (trying to watch myself like watching a movie; watching the way my brain works as if I was a compassionate friend or loved one)
6. RECOGNIZE stress and question the thinking behind it (if a thought is causing stress it is not true; tracing the thought backwards to its origins...it always seems to be trying to prove that I am worthy)
7. PARTICIPATE in healthy communities (accountability partners, fellowships, organizations, retreats, events)
8. INPUT enriching experiences (literature, film, art, architecture, museums, music, service)
9. LEARNING as much as possible from everyone and everything
10. KEEP GOING in a positive direction (always moving forward; always having faith even if not feeling faith; always doing something positive; always contributing to my well-being)
11. ON THE LOOKOUT for ways to contribute to and serve the world! (leave it a better place than when I arrived)

Think like a PROTON. Always POSITIVE. :)

RETRAIN THE BRAIN: PRACTICE, PRACTICE, PRACTICE

"Without our stories [believing our thoughts], we are not only able to act clearly, kindly, and fearlessly; we are also a friend, a listener. We are people living happy lives. We are appreciation and gratitude that have become as natural as breath itself." - Byron Katie

"Don't take anything personally. Nothing others do is because of you. What others say and do is a projection of their own reality, their own dream. When you are immune to the opinions and actions of others, you won't be the victim of needless suffering." - Don Miguel Ruiz

"You have to keep resting your mind on a positive experience for it to shape your brain." - Rick Hanson PhD

"If you love your thoughts, you love to be alone anywhere with them; you don't have to turn on the radio when you get in the car, or the tv when you get home. The way you relate to your thoughts - that's what you bring to every relationship you have, including the one with yourself." - Byron Katie

"Stop talking, stop thinking, and there is nothing you will not understand." - Seng Ts'an

"We are all visitors on this planet. During this period we must try to do something good. Something useful with our lives." - Dalai Lama

"The brain is a physical system that, like a muscle, gets stronger the more you exercise it. So make taking in the good a regular part of your life. This will be deliberate at first, but it will become increasingly automatic. Hardly thinking about it, you'll be weaving good experiences into your brain." - Rick Hanson PhD

"Earth's crammed with heaven." - Elizabeth Barrett Browning

"Listen deeply and speak lovingly." - Thich Nhat Hanh

"The present moment is filled with joy and happiness. If you are attentive, you will see it." - Thich Nhat Hanh

"It is possible to live 24 hours a day in a state of love." - Buddha

"Virtuous thoughts bring us happiness. Instead of separating us and making us feel more cut off and afraid, they bring us closer to others." - Pema Chödrön

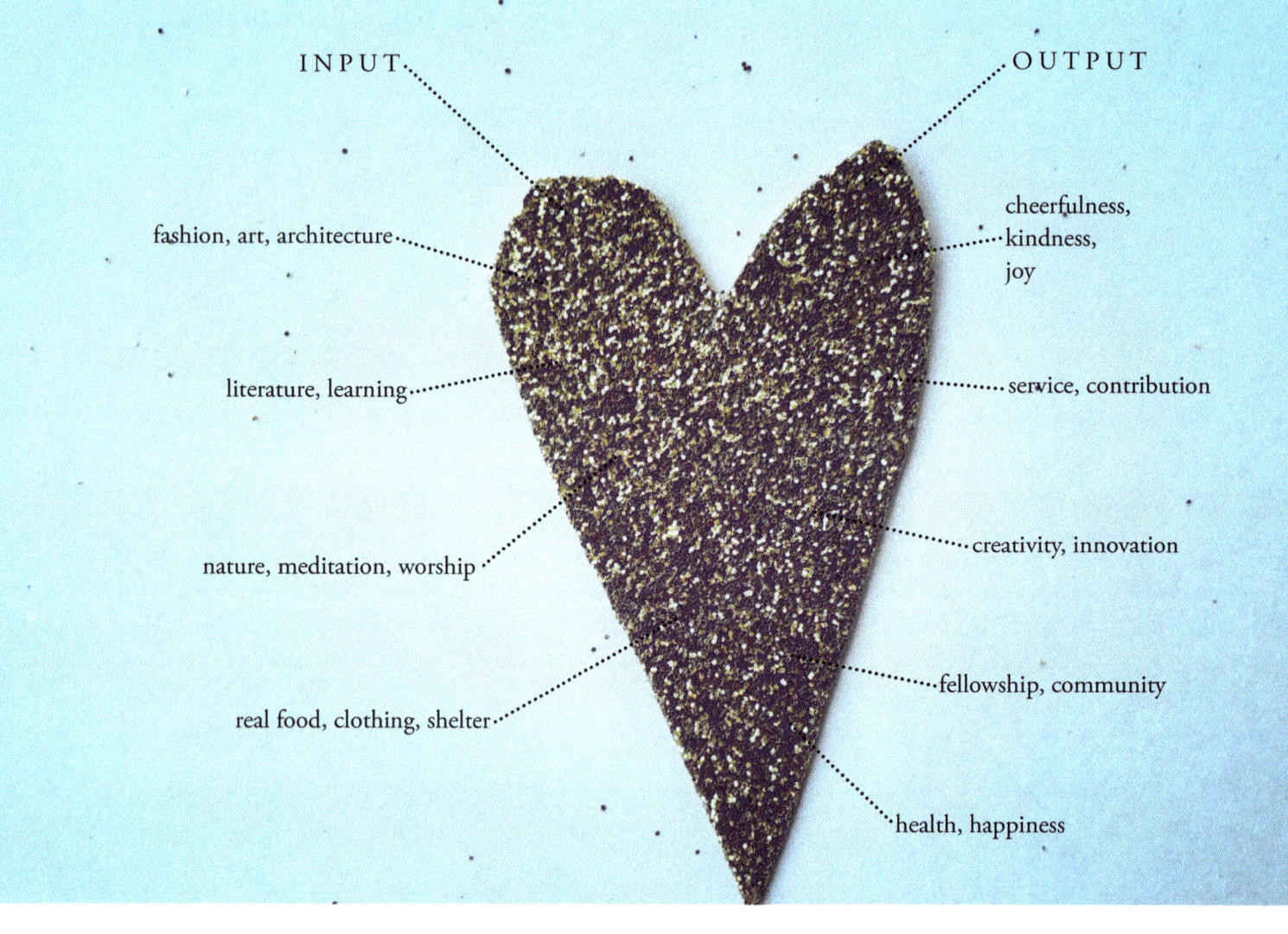

INPUT THE AWE-INSPIRING AND DIVINE

OUTPUT THE AWE-INSPIRING AND DIVINE

LIFE-CHANGING LEARNING

Martha Beck: "Imagine a place where there is nothing to fear and all your dreams have come true." (If you live life choosing moment by moment whatever feels most freeing, you will live your best life)

don Miguel Ruiz: don't take anything personally; be impeccable with your word

Eckhart Tolle: learn from animals (be a dog!): stressless, in the moment, enthusiastic, always loving, no problems!

Byron Katie: everything is exactly perfect how it is

Deepak Chopra: if you are awake when you want to be sleeping keep your eyes closed (pretend to sleep)

Thich Nhat Hahn: people taking simpler jobs in order to experience peace, equanimity, joy, simplicity, stresslessness to improve the quality of life; meditation can be staying in the moment while eating, drinking, going to the bathroom...anything!

Wayne Dyer: "there are no problems!"

Cate Shanahan and *Nora Gedgaudas*: nature produces perfect symmetry; food knowledge was secretive and sacred and passed down within groups of people (tribes/families); taste and nutrition and healthiness directly relate to the diets of the animals; symmetrical faces, fully developed jaws/eye sockets/etc humans are formed because of complete nutrition for the fetus and the nutrition of both parents up to 6 months before conception

World Book: caribou in the Tundra travel many miles each year to reach the special plants produced for a few weeks of the year in the permafrost; caribou meat provides the artic people almost all of the necessary nutrients

several sources: dogs became domesticated because humans fed them the muscle meat of the hunted animal

Mark Sisson: 80% of weight is what you eat with only 20% exercise; sleep in total darkness and install f.lux/wear yellow lenses/use yellow light bulbs; big shoes can cause injuries; over working-out can cause harm
Gary Taubes: eating fat does not make me fat
Weston Price Foundation: throughout time people from all over the world had sacred foods they would go to great lengths to find for the humans of child-bearing age
Sally Fallon and others: processed food is not food
Maria Emmerich: sleep to lose weight; eat fat; you will always be hungry without nutrients
the French: there is no food in U.S. supermarkets! impeccable ingredients
Tom Colicchio: *Think Like a Chef*
Julia Child: don't make excuses about what you've cooked; keep the chicken tasting like chicken (real chicken)

George Lois: do the work and then work some more
Jennifer L. Scott: 10-item wardrobe; connoisseur; cultivate
Marie Kondo: only have belongings that you absolutely LOVE (that speak to your heart in some way)
Richard Rohr: time limit for purpose; simplicity suggestions; pray each day for something to humble me
Stephen Fried: "If you're bored it is because you're boring."

"The clearest way into the universe is through a forest wilderness. Sermons in stones, storms, trees, flowers, and animals. Life seems neither long nor short, and we take no more heed to save time or make haste than do the trees and stars. This is true freedom..." - John Muir

We all know at some level when we cause harm to ourselves. It goes against the blueprint of all our cells: the will to stay alive and thrive. We must learn to listen impeccably to the voice of our soul. The divine spark that is other than mind or body. Failure to do so results in stress: the warning signal to change our behavior.

soul voice = instinct for self preservation; our birthright; the divinity within; the part of us that is eternal

STRESSLESSNESS

"Manage stress levels with plenty of sleep, play, sunlight, fresh air, and creative outlets and by avoiding trauma that often arises from stupid mistakes, rebel against the tremendous cultural movement toward sedentary lifestyles, excessive digital stimulation, and insufficient rest. Honor your primal genes by slowing down and simplifying your life. Your ancestors worked hard to survive, but their regular respites from stress gave them the peace of mind and body that are so highly coveted today." - Mark Sisson

"Any positive emotion is an opportunity to enjoy living and to feel satisfied here and now. Positive emotions also have many physical health benefits, including boosting your immune system, protecting your cardiovascular system, and increasing the odds of a long life. Possible good feelings: interest, eagerness, inspiration, success, abundance, cheerfulness, exhilaration, carefreeness, bliss, lightheartedness, awe, joy, feeling fortunate or blessed." - Rick Hanson PhD

"A good life consists of a lot of good days. Will you hear nature's inspirational messages? How many ads have you seen for theme parks while seeing none for public parks, where the theme is nature, beauty, and history? Will you take the time to appreciate your world...and all of its inhabitants?" - Ron Lizzi

"To live fully means lowering the risk for all disease and maximizing health at the cellular level. So many choices we make and things we encounter every day of our lives will impact our ability to live fully until we die. These include what we choose to eat and drink, where we sleep, what we put on our skin, and how we clean our homes." - Dr Myron Wentz & Dave Wentz

all-time happiness all the time

HAPPINESS TRICKS

1. Natural sleep: uninterrupted; total darkness; natural-materials mattress and bedding; wool comforter for body temperature regulation; wake naturally without an alarm; make a committment and keep the committment to getting 8-10 hours almost every night during the year; bedroom without electronics (JUST DO IT!!!); sleeping without any light exposure (even a flash of light can affect your melatonin); control thought exposure during the day (negative input can cause stressful dreams and sleep); activity/regular exercise/fresh air induce better restful sleep; magnesium spray at night; lavender aromatherapy (dried flowers under pillow)
2. Natural food: eat with purpose; feed the brain healthy fats and the whole food nutrients it craves
3. Natural clothing: dress with purpose; protect the body from toxins; keep it warm and cool while expressing the spirit
4. Natural shelter: live in nature - literally and figuratively; spend much time outdoors; bring the indoors outside (work station on the porch); bring the outdoors inside (decorate with bark, sand, stones, wood, rock grids, crystals)
5. EVERY belonging has a purpose and is the most beautiful and beloved belonging
6. Consumables: consume food, consume clothing (wear until unwearable and then use for rugs and rags), consume shoes (biodegradable), books (peruse from the library, buy if certain, tear out single pages to keep, share, give away, donate, leave purposefully as an anonymous gift)
7. Standing desks
8. Getting up each morning and going in a positive direction
9. Doing something you don't want to do every day
10. Producing something each day even if it is just a smile for someone
11. Reaching out to another human being
12. Smiling at another human being even yourself
13. Faith isn't feeling it is doing

HAPPINESS IS MY RELIGION

I remember reading from several sources but especially Byron Katie and Sri Nisargadatta Maharaj that there are no problems. Once I knew that this was possible I became determined to find it for myself. I kept reading, rereading, practicing and repeating practicing to retrain my brain. With daily diligence, I continue to experience increasing and soaring happiness!

"Your life follows your attention. Wherever you look, you end up going." - Martha Beck

"How we spend our days...is how we spend our lives." - Annie Dillard

"Happiness is your birthright...and you have access to that as long as you are breathing." - Pharrell Williams

"Happiness is your birthright - and it is readily available at any given moment." - Pema Chödrön

"Just one mental shift-focusing on the abundance of your environment-switches your psychological settings so that your life automatically improves in many areas you may think are unrelated. This is essentially a leap from fear to faith." - Martha Beck

"A lover of what is looks forward to everything: life, death, disease, loss, earthquakes, bombs, anything the mind might be tempted to call 'bad.' Life will bring us everything we need, to show us what we haven't undone yet. Nothing outside ourselves can make us suffer. Except for our unquestioned thoughts, every place is paradise."
- Byron Katie

"Life, death, preservation, loss, failure, success, poverty, riches, worthiness, unworthiness, slander, fame, hunger, thirst, cold, heat - these are the alternations of the world, the workings of fate. Day and night they change place before us, and wisdom cannot spy out their source. Therefore, they should not be enough to destroy your harmony; they should not be allowed to enter the storehouse of the spirit. If you can harmonize and delight in them, master them and never be at a loss for joy; if you can do this day and night without break and make it be spring with everything, mingling with all and creating the moment within your own mind - this is what I call being whole in power." - Zhuangzi

"in my world, nothing ever goes wrong" - Sri Nisargadatta Maharaj

MORE

Buen Camino Good Way in Life & to the End of the World book

365 Days of Happiness A Lifetime of Joy book

#myhappylifeforsale blog

cards, magnets, products, coaching

www.laurapaulisich.com

www.myhappylifeforsale.com

YouTube, Instagram, Pinterest, Twitter, Goodreads, Facebook, Google+

Laura Paulisich has a Bachelor of Arts in English from the University of Minnesota, a Master of Arts in Teaching from the University of Wisconsin, and has completed Martha Beck Life Coach Training. She lives her happy life in Hudson, Wisconsin with her dogs Aphrodite and Rumi.

www.ingramcontent.com/pod-product-compliance
Lightning Source LLC
Chambersburg PA
CBHW061151010526
44118CB00026B/2939